L IVING IN A LARGER WORLD

The Life of Murray S. Kenworthy

Leonard S. Kenworthy

Friends United Press
Richmond, Indiana

ii

Library of Congress Cataloging-in-Publication Data

Kenworthy, Leonard Stout, 1912–
    Living in a larger world.

    Includes index.
        1. Kenworthy, Murray S., 1874–1951. 2. Society of Friends—United
States—Clergy—Biography. I. Title.
BX7795.K43K46   1986   289.6'3 [B]   86-31987
ISBN 0-913408-93-X

CONTENTS

PREFACE

As I edited Volume I of *Living in the Light: Some Quaker Pioneers of the 20th Century,* I realized even more than before the pivotal part that my father, Murray S. Kenworthy, played in American Quakerism during the first five decades of this century.

Family modesty prevented me from including a chapter on him in that volume, appropriate as it would have been. Hence this account might be considered a supplementary chapter to that volume, even though it is a separate publication.

Through his life one can catch a glimpse into almost every aspect of American Quakerdom in that long period. He was associated with almost all of the major movements and organizations of that fifty-year span as Friends tried to adjust to the new world of their day and to make contributions to a better life for everyone–at home and abroad.

Many of the histories of American Quakerdom have been written from the viewpoint of Eastern Friends. I hope that this volume will add a little to the story of midwestern Quakerism, promote a balance and contribute to better understanding among the various groups of American Friends.

In this book there are brief explanations of a few events in the history of Quakerism in the United States which need to be recorded before those of us who know something about them pass from this scene. Two of them are the controversy at Earlham College early in this century in which Elbert Russell and Murray Kenworthy were the chief figures and the difficulties in Washington, D.C. when Herbert Hoover was elected President of the United States.

I hope that most readers will enjoy the entire book. I am aware, however, that the range of topics is wide, and I trust that many people will find some parts of this volume of special interest–whether it is the account of New London, Indiana, as a typical midwestern Quaker community, the story of the relief work done by English and American Friends in the Soviet Union in the 1920s, or the development of

Earlham College in the first half of this century. For those interested in the sources for this biographical account, attention is called to the material on that subject in the last part of this volume.

Although I have tried to hew as close to the line of history as possible, I may have erred here and there in depicting persons, places, events, and institutions because of the lack of adequate source materials. Where that is the case, I beg the indulgence of the readers.

In writing this account, I have had the help of several individuals. I want especially to thank Elton Trueblood from whose tribute to Murray Kenworthy I took the title of this book; my brothers Carroll and Wilmer Kenworthy; Ira Beth Kelley of the Wilmington Quaker Collection; Albert Fowler, Associate Director of the Swarthmore College Quaker Collection; and Jack Sutters, the Director of the Archives Division of the American Friends Service Committee.

As in all such volumes, I assume the full responsibility for what appears in these pages.

Leonard S. Kenworthy
Kendal at Longwood
Kennett Square, Pennsylvania

INTRODUCTION

If one person were selected to represent the multifaceted story of American Quakerdom in the first five decades of the twentieth century, that person might well be Murray S. Kenworthy. It is certainly true that Rufus M. Jones, Clarence E. Pickett, Henry J. Cadbury, and Elbert Russell were better known, especially outside the Religious Society of Friends. Yet, in many ways the life of Murray Kenworthy may represent even better the stresses and strains (and the successes) in American Quakerism in the first half of this century.

Murray Kenworthy came from a small Quaker community in Indiana. He was graduated from Earlham College and the Harvard Divinity School–rare accomplishments for anyone around the turn of this century. During World War I he was the director of the first camp for conscientious objectors. Then, after that war, he was in charge of the relief work of English and American Friends in the Soviet Union. He was also the director of the first regional office of the American Friends Service Committee, the first chairman of the Friends Committee on National Legislation, and the first head of the Rural Life Association. For a short period he was a staff member of the National Council for the Prevention of War.

Furthermore, he was executive secretary of Wilmington Yearly Meeting and of Indiana Yearly Meeting when it was the largest aggregation of Friends in the United States. From the time he was the youngest delegate to the conference which established the Five Years Meeting (now the Friends United Meeting) until his death, he was active in almost all phases of its work. But he was a pioneer in reaching out to other groups of American Quakers and in helping to foster the worldwide Religious Society of Friends, especially through his work with the American Friends Board of Foreign Missions and his participation in the First and Second World Conferences of Friends.

Murray Kenworthy was a proponent of the social gospel and of modern interpretations of the Bible, consonant with the findings of science, and he paid a price for his pioneering, being bitterly attacked and ousted from his teaching post at Earlham College. He was later vindicated and became a recognized bridge-builder between fundamentalists and modernists.

As Elton Trueblood has written, "When Quakers were beginning to be serious about the enlargement of their horizons, Murray Kenworthy was a true pioneer. He made lasting contributions in many areas. He was not satisfied to live in a small world; he lived in a larger world than most people in his day."

This book is a brief account of the life of Murray S. Kenworthy and his enlarging world. But it is more than that; it is also the story of a large segment of American Quakerdom in the first five decades of the twentieth century.

ARLY YEARS ON A HOOSIER FARM

Murray Shipley Kenworthy was born on June 28, 1874, in a farmhouse in the Quaker community of New London, Indiana. His journey into this world was a hazardous one, nearly costing the lives of mother and son.

In the light of his future, it may be worthwhile to mention that he was born on a First-Day or Sunday. Much more significant is the fact that he was named for a well-known traveling Friends minister from Cincinnati, Ohio, who had visited New London just before Murray's birth and had had a powerful impact on that community.

Murray was the first son of Milton Kenworthy and Hannah Stout Kenworthy. Family genealogy, by Carroll Kenworthy, indicates that Murray's ancestors originated in Warwickshire, near the Kenilworth Castle, in the western part of England, and that they probably were descended from the Saxons of northwestern Europe.

Murray's immediate ancestors were Kenworthys, Kirks, Stouts, and Stanfields. For generations they had been Quakers. They came to the New World in colonial times, some of them shortly after the arrival of William Penn and those early Friends who came from England on the *Welcome*, a ship which should be almost as famous as the *Mayflower*.

That boat landed in what is now Delaware in 1682. Some of its passengers spent the first winter in caves and makeshift dwellings before moving on to Philadelphia.

We know that there were Kenworthys of our family in Lancaster, Pennsylvania, in 1735, and it is possible that some of that group had lived earlier in New Jersey or in Pennsylvania. Like many other early settlers in Penn's colony, however, some of them soon moved south, primarily to Virginia and North Carolina. Others moved directly west— to Ohio and on to Indiana, or directly to Indiana. Such was the saga of those early settlers. Later some of them continued the westward migration by going to Iowa, Kansas, and California.

Many of the Stouts, particularly, settled in North Carolina. But their abhorrence of slavery led them, along with other Friends, to leave that location and head west. Entire meetings sometimes moved to the "free territory" of the old Northwest. With them they would take the minute books of their monthly meeting and even name their new community in Ohio or Indiana after their former home in the south. Two such examples are the New Garden communities in North Carolina and in Indiana, and the Rich Square communities in North Carolina and in Indiana.

Willis Kenworthy (Murray's grandfather) was the first of that branch of the family to move to New London, going there in order that his children might enjoy the education provided by Friends. Willis purchased 160 acres in that community, and it was on a farm of eighty acres which Milton Kenworthy owned that Murray was born.

Illness plagued many of those early settlers in Indiana, and some moved from place to place, hoping to improve the health of some member of their family, often the woman of the house. Thus Milton Kenworthy moved soon after the birth of Murray and the younger brother, Earl, to Missouri, calculating that a change in the climate would improve Hannah Stout's health. But he soon discovered that that was not the case, and they returned to New London.

In the prime of life, Milton Kenworthy was a short, chunky man weighing about 190 pounds. He had more energy than usual; his second wife Lucy said of him, "Pa walks with all four arms and legs." He was also very industrious and very healthy, despite the rigorous and demanding life then of a farmer. In fact, he lived to be 89.

Born on a farm near Raysville, Indiana, he had only the equivalent of three or four years of formal schooling, picked up in "winter sessions" in country schools. But he read regularly as an adult and thus compensated for his lack of a formal education. His chief fare was the local newspaper; farm papers like *The Country Gentleman, The Farm*

Journal, and the *Hoosier Farmer;* the *Bible;* and *The American Friend.*

As a boy he was extremely shy. But as a young man he knew who he wanted to court and marry–Hannah Stout. She was a most attractive redhaired girl who was the favorite with many lads in the New London community. Somehow he persuaded her to let him "walk her home" from church one Sunday night and then to go on sleigh rides with him. Not long after that they were married, when Milton was 21. To them were born three sons–Murray, Earl, and J. Willis. J. Willis lived only a few months. His death probably was caused by the carelessness of a hired helper in handling the milk supply and milk bottles when Hannah was not well enough to see to those essentials of cleanliness.

For the Kenworthys, as for their neighbors, life was filled with the farm work, with visiting with relatives and friends, and with the local Quaker meeting for worship on First and Fifth days. For the boys, as they grew older, there was school in the village of New London.

The spring before Hannah Stout Kenworthy died was a grim one for the Kenworthys. When it was clear that she would not live long, Milton tried to tell Murray what lay ahead. But the full impact of what he said was not understood by the twelve-year old boy. He did realize that there was trouble, because he was left to do much of the farm work while his father cared for his mother.

Hannah died in June, 1887, and at the funeral the members of the immediate family sat on the facing benches in the front of the meeting-house, as was the custom in those times. But that insensitive practice of exposing the family to the entire meeting so incensed Milton that he protested at a subsequent monthly meeting. Others agreed with him, and thereafter members of the family were seated at funerals in the main part of the meeting, although near the front.

That winter Milton tried to keep the little family together, with the aid of hired help. Murray did much of the housework, including making butter which was so good that people purchased it, thus adding to the family's fund. Not all of the hired helpers were competent, and they could certainly not be expected to replace a mother. So, Murray went to live with the Hoovers, next-door neighbors, and then with his Uncle Lewis and Aunt Annie Stout. Meanwhile Milton and Earl moved into New London to live with Willis Kenworthy.

Later, with Milton's marriage to Lucy Newlin, the family situation vastly improved. Of course there were adjustments to make, but Lucy was no stranger. She lived less than two miles away and belonged to the New London Friends Meeting. Before her marriage she had been teaching in the schools of Kokomo, the county seat, ten miles away. At one point, previously, Murray had been a pupil of hers in the local school.

Lucy was an excellent housekeeper and a superior cook. Family legend, however, says that Milton taught her to make "light bread" because she had been accustomed to making soda biscuits for her father. She excelled in such items as fried chicken, angel food cake, ground–cherry pies, and many other dishes. She was well-dressed and well-groomed, almost fastidious about her appearance. In fact, Murray said that if he had any complaints against her, it was that she was overly careful, perhaps a bit "prim."

In addition, she was ambitious for her sons and helped Murray with his lessons and then with his preparation for his teaching when he started that career. Every evening she and Milton read the *Bible* aloud and had family devotions. Occasionally she read aloud to him.

Lucy had a large garden which provided much of the family food. She canned everything possible in the summer, laying away food for the winter. Her part of the family exchequer came from the sale of butter, eggs, and chickens. She was careful in her spending, always putting aside money for the Missionary Society and other contributions, in addition to the tithe they both contributed to the meeting.

Murray was embarrassed by only two incidents which involved his new mother. She felt it was proper for young men to wear gloves and insisted that he purchase a pair. Other young men his age did not wear them, and although he resented her suggestion he dutifully wore them a couple of times to please her. Since he was to become a minister, she also thought it was appropriate for him to have a frock coat. That, too, irked him, and he occasionally recalled that situation in later life, referring to his embarrassment about it.

In a written account of his childhood, however, he wrote:

> But she was a *good* mother and I owe her far more than I can estimate. All the years I was away from home, she wrote me regularly, practically every week...Would that every mother going into a home in the way she did, could be as *great* a mother.

Throughout their lives this remarkable couple held a central position in the Friends meeting and in the New London community. Milton held almost every position in the meeting, serving many years as a Sunday School teacher and superintendent, as treasurer, as clerk of the ministry and oversight committee and then the pastoral committe, and as quarterly meeting clerk. He also sat "at the head of meeting" for much of his life, even though there was a pastor. He was also a township trustee when they were important local officials, in charge of the schools, the roads, and the poor.

Lucy, not as prominent in a public way, was a faithful attender and a generous contributor to the Women's Missionary Society, the Women's Christian Temperance Union, and other local groups. Almost all of the traveling ministers and Friends stayed in the Kenworthy home, attesting to her good cooking and friendly hospitality.

Milton and Lucy were known to everyone in the New London community and to many people in Howard County and beyond. So respected and beloved were they that in their later years many people affectionately called them Uncle Mit and Aunt Lucy.

One of the stories about them, which is still being told, actually occurred. One fall Lucy tearfully told Milton that her wedding ring had disappeared. Frantically they retraced her steps for the last few hours, searching everywhere for that precious possession. It was nowhere to be found. Time and again they renewed their search in the coming days and weeks.

Then, the next spring, Lucy asked Milton to go to the garden to get some radishes and onions for their noontime meal. As he leaned down to pull an onion from the soil, he spotted something shiny. He looked again. He had been right in his guess. There was "mother's wedding ring," hugging the tiny onion. And there was joy that night in New London for the Kenworthy ring had been found at last.

When Murray Kenworthy was a boy and young man, the town of New London had forty or fifty houses, a general store which also housed the Post Office, a smaller store, the grade school and high school, a blacksmith shop, the office of a country doctor, the Town Hall, and the Friends Meeting. From time to time there was a Holiness Church, but it was not a permanent feature of the community.

At one point people felt certain that New London would be the county seat, and several streets were laid out in anticipation of that event. The remnants of those streets are visible today. But the railroad was routed through Kokomo, and natural gas was discovered near that locality. So Kokomo, named for an Indian chief, became the county seat. New London remained a small town.

The New London community, however, was more than the village; it was a large area of farms. Those farms in Howard County, as in almost all of the Old Northwest Territory, had been surveyed and laid out in a checkerboard fashion. The main unit was 640 acres, although most people purchased smaller plots of 320, 160, or 80 acres. Thus a farm could be easily located. For those who like technical terms the farm on which Milton Kenworthy settled, and on which Murray and his brother

Earl were raised, was the northeast quarter of section 12, township 23, range 2 east. (You might be completely confused by such a description or you might find it intriguing to locate.)

When Willis Kenworthy moved to the New London area, he purchased 160 acres and it was 80 of that which comprised the farm on which Milton raised his crops and his family. Contrary to the belief of many people today, such farm land was not all level and free of encumbrances. Only about half of Milton's farm had been cleared of trees and rocks, ditched and rail-fenced. There was a heavy mortgage on his place, and hog cholera and low prices plagued Milton despite his hard work and his astuteness as a farmer. In addition, Hannah was not well, having contracted what was called in those days "consumption." So there were doctor's bills, expenses for medicines, and the wages for the hired help, as well as taxes.

Consequently, life was not easy for Milton Kenworthy and the other farmers of that period and place. As Murray wrote in an autobiographical account which he started at the behest of his sons near the end of his life:

> Few of the present generation realize the enormous amount of work that was necessary to clear the forests, remove the boulders, drain the fields, and build the fences—all in addition to the other work of ploughing, planting, and harvesting. No wonder, then, that men were often old at 40.

The house in which Murray lived as a boy was typical of Hoosier farm homes of that period—one-and-a-half wooden buildings made from the oak, poplar, walnut, ash, or maple trees nearby. In the Kenworthy home was a fireplace in the living room, but the house was heated by wood stoves. In the winter the family huddled around those fires in the kitchen and living room. As babies and young children, Murray and Earl slept in trundle beds which could be slipped under the bed of their parents during the day. But as they grew older, they were shunted off upstairs. That part of the house was unfinished and had no heat so it was bitter cold in the winter.

Near the house was a small barn, big enough to shelter two or three cows and two or three horses, and a woodshed which was used largely for the farm implements and other tools. A small building, half above ground and half below it, was used to store potatoes and apples; it doubled as the milk room. In addition, there was a chicken house and a place where the wood ashes were stored and where water was poured over them before making soap in a big iron kettle placed over an outdoor fire.

The Kenworthy home was located several rods from the main road–so the house could be in a dry part of the land and the horses could graze and roll on a big front lawn. Horses in that time were especially prized if they could turn over on the ground, raise their feet high into the air, and even turn back again.

The soil on Milton Kenworthy's farm was relatively good, but there were still many acres to clear when Murray was a boy. That was slow, difficult, and sometimes dangerous work. There were also stumps to be removed, burned, or ploughed around. Giant boulders, left from the time of the glaciers, needed to be removed. Some could be hauled away by the horses; some could be buried. But others could be disposed of only by piling large amount of debris around them, lighting the pile, and then dashing water on it to split the rocks.

In addition, the land had to be drained. That meant digging ditches and laying pipes or conduits, made at first of wood and later of tile. A farmer could only lay around eighty rods of pipes a year, so it was a long time before the entire eighty acres could be drained.

The chief crops in the 1880s and 1890s in Howard County were corn, wheat, oats, and clover. Clover was the only crop which produced two yields a summer. The first was used for hay and the second for next season's seed. Occasionally a farmer would grow flax, buckwheat, millet, or broom corn. But these crops were rare. Many years later, Milton Kenworthy planted the first soy beans on a ten-acre plot of ground, and farmers drove for miles to see it. But soybeans were only used in those days for cattle feed or to turn over to replenish the supply of nitrogen in the soil, not for the myriad purposes for which those "wonder beans" are used today.

Work on the farm was demanding in time and in energy. Hence there was little time for play and almost no organized recreation. The nearest to organized recreation were the meals of the threshing gangs or the times when people worked together–making maple syrup, apple butter, or butchering. Of course, during Quarterly Meetings at the New London meetinghouse, relatives and friends (both a capital F and a small f) came from a few miles away and sometimes stayed overnight.

As a young lad Murray had a large gourd which he used as a drum and he had great fun marching around the yard and out into the orchard. Even that was threatened one day when one of the hired help said (probably in fun) that he was going to take that instrument from him. Murray hid and did not appear even for supper. He came out of hiding only when the adult left the house.

At Christmas time Murray and Earl hung their stockings, but the gifts were meager–a little candy and a small china toy. Once he was given a china camel which he dearly loved, and upon another occasion a mug with the words "Forget Me Not" on it–which he used as a shaving mug for most of his life.

He and Earl also had a wagon which provided them with a great deal of fun, including hauling home the walnuts they gathered in the nearby woods. Murray had some skates, but he said that he never enjoyed skating because he was forever getting blisters or raw spots on his feet from them. He also had a home-made sled with wooden runners.

When he was older, Murray sometimes played town ball (a game which was a little like baseball) with the boys at school. Similar to that was two- or three-corner cat (ball). In those games they used flatboards rather than the round bats of today.

In the summer they roamed the woods, swinging from the wild grape vines, picking paw-paws or beech nuts, or playing in the water of East Honey Creek, Little Wild Cat, or Big Wild Cat. Fishing was another diversion, and Murray and Earl occasionally indulged in it with their father.

Sometimes they went hunting for ground squirrels (striped chipmunks). For a time they hunted snakes and killed them. But when they learned that the snakes killed the field mice, Murray and Earl quit destroying them. A few times they killed quail, but they stopped doing that, too, when they learned that they helped the farmers by destroying pests.

There were few books in the Kenworthy home, but Murray recalled with gratitude the hours his father spent in reading *Uncle Tom's Cabin* aloud to Earl and him. Then, when Murray was in high school and a member of the Junta Society, he "read voraciously" according to his own account.

He remembered only one game played at home in the evening–Pussy Wants a Corner. But he did recall as an adult another enjoyable part of their family life. Here is how he once described that special form of fun:

> As I think back, we had some things which we much enjoyed that we do not have now. In a sense they were luxuries-plenty of nuts (hickory, walnut, and beech nuts) and plenty of apples. Those were mighty fine times when we gathered around the warm stove in the evening for a before-bedtime feed.

There were also some special experiences for farm boys in those days. They can hardly be described as fun, but they were fleeting pleasures for people with eyes to see, ears to hear, and hearts to take them in.

In the spring there was the feel and smell of the newly turned earth under one's bare feet and the sight of the recently planted corn or wheat shyly sending up shoots through the soil. In the same season there was the pleasure of watching the birds build their nests and seeing the parents teaching the fledglings to fly–bluebirds and blue jays, robins, red-winged blackbirds, bob-o-links, quails or pheasants, and others. Throughout his life Murray loved to watch birds.

In the late spring and summer there were the glorious sights of the vast expanses of wheat blowing to and fro and forming variegated patterns as the wind played hide and seek in the fields. And often the sun shone on the dew-soaked cobwebs in the morning. There were raspberries and blackberries, paw-paws, and beech nuts to pluck and eat–sometimes on the run.

In the fall there were flaming red maples and various shades of yellow, orange, and russet of the oaks and tulip poplars. There was the crunch of dried leaves as one scurried through them on the way to school or to the woods. Trees were one of Murray's specialties, and he knew them well by their leaves and by their bark.

There were sunrises and sunsets in all seasons, too, as well as an occasional rainbow trying to lure people to search for the pot of gold supposedly hidden at the end of that heavenly band of color. Farm life was often demanding and dangerous, but it had its compensations.

THE NEW LONDON QUAKER COMMUNITY

In *Friends for 300 Years*, Howard Brinton described the golden age of American Quakerism as the period from 1700 to 1740 in the Middle Colonies. In that period and in that part of the colonies he maintained that there was "a distinctive Quaker culture," a way of life that permeated every aspect of those communities.

Friends would settle in a region and immediately build a meeting-house. In it they would often hold school, as well as convening meetings for worship and meetings for business. Then, as soon as possible, they would construct a separate schoolhouse nearby. In one of those buildings there would be a small library.

The poor would be cared for by the meeting, and disputes and delinquencies were settled in the meeting for business or by the elders. There also was an economic dimension to such communities: the members depended strongly on each other and often built their homes and harvested their crops together. There were social times, too, especially at quarterly meeting sessions when Friends from a distance would be entertained in the homes of local Quakers.

What Howard Brinton described for that period and that part of the colonies was duplicated in many Quaker communities in various parts of the United States far into the nineteenth century. New London, Indiana, had most of those characteristics of a Quaker community and culture; its distinctive way of life permeated almost every aspect of everyday living. Hoosier historians and the records of Friends meetings indicate that the community arose in the 1840s, largely as a result of the convergence of two streams of migration in Howard County, about seventy-five miles north of the present capital city of Indianapolis. One stream flowed from the Whitewater region (Richmond) in the east; the other from White Lick in the west. Probably a third emerged from the southern part of what became the state of Indiana in 1816.

Like the Quakers in other parts of Indiana, these Friends or their ancestors had come from North Carolina and Tennessee, from Pennsylvania and Ohio. Some of them came directly; others stopped for a few years enroute to Howard County.

Those from the southern part of the United States abhorred the slavery system there and were fleeing from it. They moved to Indiana and other parts of the Old Northwest Territory because the Ordinance of 1787 declared that region to be henceforth free from slavery. (Daniel Webster even went so far as to call the Northwest Ordinance "the most liberty-loving document ever written in human history.") Apparently New London was not settled until the 1840s because some of the area had been used by the Indians and because some of the land was water-logged and therefore not promising for farming. Anyway, the Quakers came and have stayed to this day.

Enough Friends had settled in the New London area in 1845 to form a preparative Quaker meeting known as Honey Creek. Poplar Grove Preparative Meeting was formed in 1846. And in 1846 those two groups formed one monthly meeting, called Honey Creek. They met alternately in the two places until 1849 when they met only at Honey Creek (New London).

Meanwhile Western Yearly Meeting had been "set up" by Indiana Yearly Meeting in 1857. Western was composed of meetings in the Western part of Indiana and the eastern part of Illinois. In 1862, during the Civil War, Honey Creek Quarterly Meeting was established. Its first clerks were John Newlin and Silas Stout, ancestors of Lucy Newlin and Hannah Stout (the first and second wives of Milton Kenworthy). It was not until 1892 that the name of the quarterly meeting was changed to New London, the name it still holds.

The first meetinghouse in what is now New London was built as soon as the new settlers could construct it. It became too small, and a new frame building was built and completed in 1853, with a seating capacity of nearly one thousand. It was a typical Friends meetinghouse for those days. Men and women attended the meetings for worship on First and Fifth Days together, but the shutters between the two sides of the room were closed for the separate business meetings of the two sexes. That practice may seem strange today, but it had developed in order to give women fuller participation in the life of the meeting. This resulted throughout Quakerdom in giving women the experience of running business meetings, which proved so helpful in their leadership in the women's rights movement.

In 1903, a third meetinghouse was built and Milton Kenworthy was one of the members of the committee in charge of its construction. That structure served the community well until 1951 when it burned and the present, more elaborate, stone building was constructed.

Until the latter part of the nineteenth century the meetings for worship were held on the basis of silence or of expectancy. Vocal ministry was largely confined to the "recorded ministers" (both men and women) and the leaders, although occasionally others would speak. Meetings were held on Fifth Day morning as well as on First Days, as a part of the continuing testimony that all days of the week are holy days. Farmers would unhitch their horses from the ploughs or stop whatever work they were doing and drive with their families to the meetinghouse for at least an hour of group worship.

During the middle decades of the nineteenth century, Quakers in New London, as elsewhere, had their special concerns—education, peace, missions, and the plight of Negroes (now referred to as blacks). Some New London Friends took part in the Underground Railroad which transported slaves north, sometimes as far away as Canada. The local station on that famous railroad was the blacksmith's shop. The room above the shop was heated by the fire below, making it livable for the transients.

During the latter part of the nineteenth century the winds of change were blowing in Indiana, as in other parts of the country, and the original form of Quaker worship on the basis of expectant silence was gradually being altered. Much of that occurred during the childhood and youth of Murray Kenworthy and vitally affected his later life. The reasons for the rise of programmed meetings and the hiring of pastors are more numerous and involved than is often realized.

Almost all Friends in New London were farmers, and the men, in particular, were alone a large part of the time. Silence was built into their lives. Linked with this was the fact that most Quakers there, as elsewhere, had only a basic education, did not read much and could not afford to travel. Consequently, when they went to meeting they were ready, even eager, for the spiritual stimulation of spoken ministry.

Undoubtedly some of the messages in meeting were moving. But they were infrequent. Often the ministry was dull, uninspiring, repetitious, and exhortative rather than educational and edifying. There were meetings, too, where there were no messages–just the silence. Those silent periods could provide a fertile time for soul-searching, healing, hope, and inspiration. But if Friends truly believe that God speaks through people as well as to them, there should be some Divinely-inspired speaking.

Occasionally there was a visit from a traveling Friend. He or she often brought new and fresh messages or at least an unfamiliar voice. But there were many meetings for such ministers to visit. New London had more than its share of such newcomers because it was a large and well-known Quaker center. Yet even there such visits were few and far between. Even the social pressure for attending meeting did not prevent some people from absenting themselves, and the meeting began to decline.

In the wider world, the Great Revival Movement was taking place across large parts of the United States. Evangelists drew large crowds, and the choirs and congregational singing provided an emotional background for their preaching. Large numbers of people were "saved," and often their lives were altered.

In the churches of such groups the singing attracted young people. Many of them enjoyed the feeling of "belonging" that participation in choirs provided. In addition, there were Sunday Schools and eventually Cbristian Endeavor Societies, both tailored to meet the needs of boys and girls and young people. Through a combination of such factors the congregations of the Methodists, the Baptists, and other Protestant groups grew while the Quaker meetings dwindled.

Discouraged by the moribund ministry and their decline in membership, many Friends looked with envy on the growth of other groups. So, in a sincere, desperate, and sometimes misguided search for survival and renewal, Friends began to emulate the methods of other religious groups rather than developing authentic Quaker ways for revival.

Sunday Schools were started in which music played an important part, and the materials used as texts were produced almost exclusively by non-Friends. Later, Christian Endeavor Societies were launched in which young people could take active leadership roles. Friends joined with other groups in sponsoring revival meetings, or they held their own, often with evangelists from other denominations in charge. Frequently many people responded to the altar calls and started to come to Quaker meetings. They found the meetings on the basis of silence vastly different from the revival services they had attended, so they asked for more preaching, music, and a much more evangelical and emotional approach to religion.

Meanwhile non-Friends moved into what had been predominately Quaker communities, and if they were to be attracted to the meeting, some changes needed to be made. Young people also began to ask for music in the meeting. If it was appropriate in the First Day School or Sunday School, why not in the meeting for worship?

In New London changes occurred gradually. Most of them took place when Murray Kenworthy was a boy and a young man. Music was introduced in the early part of the meeting for worship. Then it was felt that it would be better music and more inspiring if there was a choir. So a choir was organized, usually composed of young people. In order to improve the vocal ministry, the meeting hired a pastor and, to supplement a meager salary, provided a parsonage. Because the periods of silence were not long enough to develop messages from the members, they were reduced radically in length, sometimes becoming almost a perfunctory "few moments of silence." As a result of such changes, non-Friends in the community often were attracted to the meeting and sometimes joined it.

Thus the unprogrammed meeting became a semi-programmed meeting and then a programmed meeting. Brief periods of silence or an "open" part of the worship were maintained, however, and for many years a member of the Committee on Ministry and Oversight (later the Pastoral Committee) sat with the pastor "at the head of the meeting."

Over the period of several decades the New London Friends Meeting has remained about the same size, with a membership of around two hundred (including non-residents), and with an attendance of one hundred or so at Sunday School and seventy-five to eighty-five at the meeting for worship.

Undoubtedly Murray heard many discussions on Quakerism and on the contemplated changes in the New London Meeting. He probably took part in some of them, as his immediate family and nearly all of his relatives, neighbors, and friends attended there.

Early in life, around the age of ten, Murray decided he would become a minister, and in his teens he occasionally took part in the "open period" of the meeting for worship. In the autobiographical account which he started to write late in his life, he recorded something of his early religious expriences:

> I do not recall any time of definite "conversion," although I do
> recall going to the altar several times during revival meetings,

not from any personal need but because it was the accepted thing to do. If there was any "change" in my life, presumably it was because of the general atmosphere in our home.

He attended Sunday School and was one of the charter members of the local Christian Endeavor Society. He was possibly influenced, too, by at least two relatives who were ministers. One was his Uncle Amos Kenworthy, a very prominent Quaker minister about whom a biography has been written and about whom California Yearly Meeting produced a pamphlet in the 1970s in its Quaker Leaders Series. Amos Kenworthy traveled far and wide among Friends and was one of the best-known Quakers of that generation. More important might have been the influence of Murray's grandfather, Willis, who was a recorded minister in the New London Meeting and later a farmer and part-time pastor of the Amboy, Indiana, Friends Meeting. Willis Kenworthy, however, urged Murray to become a teacher.

Actually Murray became both a teacher and a minister. But in 1897, at the age of twenty-three, he was "recorded" by Friends, which means that they considered that he had a "gift in the ministry." That was an early age at which to be recorded, so there must have been general agreement. He had not yet completed his work at Earlham College, although he stayed out of school a few years in order to teach and thus earn enough money to complete his education.

Within the New London community the Kenworthy and Stout families produced at least eight ministers in three or four generations. In addition to Amos, Willis, and Murray, there was Murray's Uncle Allen Kenworthy (later a Methodist minister), and four cousins–the most widely known being Lewis Stout and Lyman Cosand. But that small community produced several other prominent Friends who served in a much larger area than that one locality. William and Chester Reagan both spent a part of their youth in New London when their father, Jehu Reagan, was a pastor. "Will" Reagan was the principal of Oakwood School in Poughkeepsie, New York, for many years, while Chester Reagan was the last principal of the Spiceland Academy in Indiana (while it was still a Quaker insitiution) and then was principal of the Moorestown (New Jersey) Friends School for many years.

Lewis and Paul Taylor were both born and brought up in New London. For several years Lewis taught at Westtown School, the boarding school of Philadelphia Yearly Meeting (Arch Street). Paul taught most of his life at Oakwood School, the New York Yearly Meeting School, until his retirement, and then at George School, the Philadelphia Yearly Meeting (Race Street) boarding school.

Caroline Nicholson was born in New London when her father was principal of the high school there and is well-known among Quakers. She taught and served as assistant principal of Westtown School, wrote several books on Quakerism, and was clerk of Southeastern Yearly Meeting. Her older brothers have also been distinguished. Vincent was the first executive secretary of the American Friends Service Committee, and Francis was an investment and trust officer for more than forty years with the Provident National Bank in Philadelphia. He also was treasurer of the Friends Fiduciary Corporation which handles the funds of many Quaker organizations and institutions along the eastern seaboard.

Two other prominent Friends who were products of New London were Norval Webb, a well-known Quaker minister and for several years the executive secretary of Western Yearly Meeting, and Florence Mills, the wife of Eldon Mills, a prominent Quaker and then Congregational minister. In her later years Florence Mills served with distinction as the secretary of the Wilmington (Delaware) Friends Meeting.

New London also made its contribution to education. It is important to remind American Friends from time to time of the enormous contribution made by Quakers, wherever they lived, to the elementary schools of those localities and later to the running of Quaker academies. As mentioned earlier, Quakers always built a meetinghouse wherever they moved. Then, within a short time, they would start an elementary school.

New London, Indiana, followed that tradition when Friends from various communities and states converged there. A small school began in a log cabin in 1840 with an eccentric teacher from New York state and ten or twelve students. By 1842 the local monthly meeting had built a two-room school in the village of New London near the meetinghouse. Its student body ranged from thirty to seventy pupils, depending upon the year. In 1864, a secondary school, The New London Academy, was opened under the care of the quarterly meeting. It met in a three-room frame building.

Now there were two Quaker schools in the community, the elementary school run by the monthly meeting and the secondary school run by the quarterly meeting.

The New London Academy was by no means the only such institution run by Friends in Indiana in the nineteenth century, and in a few cases into the twentieth. In 1868 there were nineteen such secondary schools. In 1883, there were only eleven because the state was developing free, public high schools. Three of those very special schools run by Friends lasted until the 1920s and 1930s–Spiceland

Academy (closed in 1922) Fairmount Academy (1924), and Vermilion Academy in Illinois (1937). The major Quaker academies in Indiana included Amboy Academy, Beech Grove Seminary, Bloomingdale Academy, Blue River Academy, Carthage Academy, Central Academy (in Plainfield), Dover School, Fairfield Academy, Fairmount Academy, Farmers Institute, Mooresville High School, New London Quarterly Meeting School, the Newport and New Garden Schools, Poplar Ridge Seminary, Rich Square Academy, Richland Academy, Rush Creek School, Sand Creek Friends Seminary, South Wabash Academy, Spiceland Academy, Sugar Plain Academy, and Union High School.

For several years the Quaker academies were the only institutions of what was then "higher education" in several states. They drew primarily on the Quaker constituency in the local community, but also attracted students from other localities and even a few from out of the state. Frequently students boarded in the homes of local people during the week, returning home over the weekend and bringing back with them fresh supplies of food for the coming week. In some schools there were boarders.

The purpose of all these schools was to provide a Christian education as interpreted by Friends. Often the term "a guarded education" was used to describe the efforts of Quakers to provide for advanced education for their children. Perhaps it is important to mention that girls as well as boys were enrolled in those institutions. Friends, from the beginning of their history in England, had started and administered schools for both sexes–at first for boys and girls separately, but very early as coeducational institutions. Eventually many non-Friends were enrolled in those schools, and in a few cases the township paid the costs of non-Friends where there was no other secondary school.

In New London the academy was sold to the township around 1874, and New London High School was organized. However, that public institution was heavily influenced by Friends and the principal and teachers were frequently Quakers.

Murray Kenworthy attended New London High School, graduating in 1892. The principal was a Quaker named S. Edgar Nicholson who became a nationally known figure late in life. After he left New London, he became a newspaper editor in Kokomo, a member of the Indiana Legislature, a prominent leader in the Anti-Saloon League in various states and its national executive secretary, an officer in the National Council for the Prevention of War in Washington, D.C., and editor of *The American Friend*. It was he who had a large part in persuading Murray Kenworthy to continue his education at Earlham College.

One special feature of New London High school for many years was the Junta Literary Society, in which Murray was active. It met in the evenings and was really associated with the school only in a minor way. It did provide opportunites for a few students to pursue their interest in literature and in debating in a way that was not possible in the ordinary curriculum. That group was responsible for starting and augmenting a good library for the high school, and they published a respectable magazine called *The Junta Star*. Aside from the Friends Meeting, the Junta Literary Society was the place where Murray gained his experience in public speaking, presiding, debating, and in extending his interest in books and writing.

Readers who are interested in memorabilia would relish the Commencement issue of May 29, 1896, of *The Junta Star* which lies before me as I type this paragraph. It is a twenty-eight page booklet which sold for ten cents and carried ads from the local merchants for binding twine, pure drugs and patent medicines, bicycles and harnesses, whips and robes, as well as the commencement essays and a history of the Junta Society written by a recent graduate, Murray S. Kenworthy.

With the changes in the Friends meeting, with the disappearance of the Quaker Academy, and such innovations as the appearance of automobiles, the tight-knit community life of New London was being altered toward the end of the nineteenth century and the beginning of the twentieth. Who can say whether those changes were for good or ill?

STUDENT DAYS AT EARLHAM COLLEGE

Probably the most important decision Murray Kenworthy ever made was to go to Earlham College. That decision started him down a highway which was quite different from the road on which he would have traveled had he remained in New London as a Quaker farmer. That move widened his world geographically, socially, educationally, religiously, philosophically, and economically.

Going to college in those days was unusual for a Hoosier farm boy, even in a Quaker community. Only one young man had done so in the New London community, and that was Murray's cousin, Elmer Stout. Possibly he had some influence on Murray's decision.

But it was two adults who really encouraged him to further his education. One was his stepmother, Lucy. She had been a school teacher before becoming a Kenworthy and valued education highly. Undoubtedly she recognized in her son some talents which should be released and cultivated. Perhaps she was living out some of her own ambitions, as so many parents do through their children. The other encourager was S. Edgar Nicholson, the principal of the New London High School. Apparently Milton neither discouraged nor encouraged Murray from going to college. Certainly he was not yet in a financial position to help his son.

Murray earned his way through college. It took seven years to complete the four-year college course. His first job was as the teacher of an elementary school near the Kenworthy farm. At another time he taught for two years in the upper four grades of the school in the nearby community of West Middleton. In the summers he worked on the family farm and as a hired hand on other farms nearby and also did some preaching in nearby Friends meetings. He cut every conceivable corner to make ends meet. For example, on at least one occasion he rode his bicycle from New London to Richmond, a distance of ninety miles, to save the cost of the train fare.

The city of Richmond to which Murray Kenworthy moved in 1892 to attend Earlham College was an unusual community, far more advanced than most towns and cities of that time in the Midwest.

A century earlier several of the original American colonies laid claim to the land west of the Appalachians. But in one of the few successes of the government under the Articles of Confederation, they all agreed to cede that land to the new national government. Under the terms of the Northwest Ordinance of 1787, plans were made for the eventual formation of states from that vast tract of land, when there were sixty thousand residents in a given area. Eventually five states were formed—Ohio, Indiana, Illinois, Michigan, and Wisconsin. For the anti-slavery forces the Northwest Ordinance was a stunning victory because it declared that "There shall be neither slavery or involuntary servitude in said territory."

That declaration about slavery in the Northwest Territory appealed to many Quakers, especially those in North Carolina, Tennessee, and other parts of the South. Abhorring slavery, they decided to emigrate from the area in which that vicious institution was legal and try their fortunes in another part of the world.

Several factors attracted them to the area around what is now Richmond. First was the fact that it was in free territory. There also was the advantage of good soil, some of it left by the glaciers that had covered that region long ago. They were drawn by the water supply of the Whitewater River and the supply of stone from its rocky cliffs.

By 1809 there were an estimated 265 Friends in the Whitewater Valley and a Whitewater Monthly Meeting was "set up." By 1821 there were enough Friends in Indiana for a yearly meeting to be "set off" from Ohio Yearly Meeting.

Those early Quakers were a God-fearing or God-loving people, marked by plain language (thees and thous), plain clothes (bonnets and broad-brimmed hats), sobriety, frugality, and industriousness. Life was not easy on that new frontier, but they worked hard and prospered.

Most of those early Friends were farmers, but there was a need for a trading center. Richmond developed in large part to serve that purpose. The town was designed in 1818. Various names were suggested for it, including Waterford and Plainfield. It finally was decided to call it Richmond, probably because the ancestors of some of the early settlers had come from Richmond County in England. In a way that name was a misnomer as it meant *rich mound* or *mountain*. Nevertheless, the name stuck. It was a popular title, too, for there are now twenty-six towns by that name in the United States.

Richmond was laid out on a checkerboard pattern with the streets north and south designated by numbers–First, Second, and Third; those east and west (for a time only) by the names of plants and trees–Sycamore, Vine, Sassafras, Walnut, and Mulberry, but later by the alphabet–A, B, C, D, etc.

The county was called Wayne, named for the famous (or infamous) warrior "Mad" Anthony Wayne in the early conflicts between the whites and the Indians. It was a strange name for an area inhabited by so many Quakers, and Wayne had nothing to do with the county named for him.

Soon there were mills for grinding grain, tanneries for making shoes and harnesses, blacksmith shops for tools and shodding the feet of horses, weavers for producing carpets and coverlets, and cabinet-making shops for making all kinds of furniture. A few years later (1839-1845) silk cloth was made locally from silk worms.

In the 1820s and 1830s Methodists and Presbyterians came to Richmond, and it began to be a more cosmopolitan community. Then, in the 1830s and 1840s Lutherans and Catholics came from Germany, bringing their love of art and music with them and complementing the Quaker contributions. Actually the Germans were so numerous that by the end of the century they constituted about one-third of the citizens of Richmond. In the 1830s, Irish came to work on the canal and some of them stayed, adding another ethnic and national group.

In the middle west in the nineteenth century, the people in many towns and villages hoped that a major highway would be routed through their locality. Some wanted a canal or hoped for a railroad. If they could obtain one of those means of transportation, they would be happy. Two would elate them. Acquiring all three was something to be sought, but seldom achieved.

Richmond, Indiana, however, was one of the rare places which eventually had all three. The National Road (running from Cumberland, Maryland to San Francisco, California) was planned in 1806 but no work was started on it until 1822. By 1827 the section of it which ran through Richmond was completed. For a few years there was also a canal from nearby Cambridge City to the Ohio river in the south, although the canal period was very brief. In 1853 Richmond obtained its first railroad-linking it to Dayton and Cincinnati in the east and Indianapolis in the west. Later Richmond became a major stop on the transcontinental line of the Pennsylvania Railroad. And when the extensive network of electric inter-urbans was developed, Richmond was linked with almost every part of Indiana and Ohio.

There was also a very different type of railroad which ran through Richmond and many other communities, one which transported slaves clandestinely from the south into free territory, often as far as Canada. It was a silent, secret, and subversive undertaking in which many Quakers participated. Known as the Underground railroad, its headquarters or hub of activity was in Fountain City, a few miles north of Richmond, and its so-called president was Levi Coffin, a prominent Quaker who hailed from North Carolina.

So Richmond became a central community, serving governmentally as the county seat (replacing Centerville in 1873), economically as the trading center of a large agricultural area, and religiously as a center of midwestern Quakerism.

Richmond grew from two hundred residents in 1818 to nearly four thousand in 1850 and to almost eighteen thousand in 1890.

True to Quaker pattern the minutes of Whitewater Monthly Meeting indicate that as early as 1810 Quakers were collecting books for use by their children. Then, in 1811-1812, they established their first Quaker elementary school. (There were no public schools yet in that part of the country.)

One of the problems all Quaker schools in the area faced was the shortage of qualified teachers. Whitewater Monthly Meeting and then the quarterly meeting began pressing for a school where Quaker children could continue their education and where teachers could be educated. That concern was voiced as early as 1829. By 1832 their proposal for starting a boarding school was brought concurrently before the men's and women's meetings of Indiana Yearly Meeting. (A sidelight on the times is the fact that in spite of the supposed equality of the sexes in Quaker circles, there were two thousand men at that yearly meeting and only one thousand women.)

Some Friends felt that higher learning would lead to a decrease in spirituality; others saw the need for more and better-prepared teachers. A few had the feeling that the Orthodox-Hicksite division (which had started in the east in 1827-1828 and then spread westward) might have been avoided if Quakers had been better educated in the Bible and in Friends' principles.

Quakers often move slowly in the decision-making process, largely in order to achieve unity. Such was the case in regard to the proposed boarding school. Eventually the decision was made to establish such an institution, and in 1833 land totaling 320 acres was purchased in West Richmond for $5,800.

Money was scarce in those days because of national economic panic and periods of financial depression. So the fund for the construction of the new building was slow in being raised. It was not until the summer session of 1847 that the Friends Boarding School opened with twenty-three boys and twenty-two girls. However, in the fall term of that year there were forty-five boys and thirty-seven girls.

The names of some of those students may be of interest to some readers as they represent prominent Quaker families in the Midwest over a period of several decades. Among them were Binford, Bond, Coffin, Davis, Evans, Furnas, Hadley, Jay, Mendenhall, Newby, Test, True-blood, White, and Wildman.

Many individuals were responsible for the creation of that forerunner of Earlham College. But the name of Elijah Coffin leads all the rest. Born in North Carolina, he was a teacher and clerk of North Carolina Yearly Meeting when he was twenty-four years old. Moving to Indiana, he was successively a storekeeper and a bank official. For twenty-six years he was superintendent of the First Day school of the Whitewater Friends Meeting and for thirty-one years the presiding clerk of Indiana Yearly Meeting. The Friends Boarding School was the culmination of his concern for Quaker education.

But the demand for education was increasing everywhere in the United States. One reason for more and better-trained teachers was because several Quaker academies had sprung up in Indiana. Another was the demand for better-educated individuals for the many jobs that were being created as the United States became more industrialized.

So, after prolonged discussion among the Friends of Indiana Yearly Meeting, the Friends Boarding School became Earlham College in 1859. The same transition occurred in other places: the boarding school at Haverford, Pennsylvania, became Haverford College in 1856, and the one in Greensboro, North Carolina became Guilford College in 1889. Thus the era of Quaker colleges was ushered in, with Earlham among the earliest.

When Murray Kenworthy entered Earlham in 1893, the college had a little more than two hundred students, almost equally divided between men and women. The student body had not yet become national; most of them were from nearby communties in Indiana and a large percentage were Quakers.

Like all Earlham presidents, the head of that institution was an extremely able leader, Joseph John Mills. He had attended the University of Michigan and Earlham and then headed the monthly meeting school at Valley Mills, near Indianapolis. Following that, he had been the principal and then the superintendent of schools in Wabash and the assistant superintendent of schools in Indianapolis. He was a recorded minister and had been on the Earlham Board of Trustees.

Installed in 1884, he brought about many changes in the college, strengthening its finances, building new buildings, and extending its courses of study. Although "a guarded education" was still the goal of Earlham, vocal music was permitted in 1885. About the same time art was introduced under the instruction of John Elwood Bundy, a famous artist from the Midwest. Plays, even dialogues, were prohibited, however, until 1899. Courses in religion were still required of all students, but President Mills permitted them to be used as credits for graduation, an innovation during his incumbency.

To reduce the college's debt, the one hundred acres which Earlham owned north of the National Road was sold, as well as forty-two acres south of that thoroughfare. The campus, however, was still ample for its needs. Across from the campus on the north side of the National Road was a boarding house for the Earlham Biblical Institute. In 1887 Lindley Hall was built to house the administrative offices and class-rooms. And Parry Hall had been constructed as a small science building. During Murray's days at Earlham there was still an active preparatory department as it was not terminated until 1902-1903.

The twenty Earlham faculty members were exceptionally able men and women. Compared to today's "teaching load," they were highly overworked, teaching twenty-three hours a week. In addition, they were all expected to give seven chapel and public lectures each academic year.

Perhaps the most notable member of the faculty was Joseph Moore, after whom the present museum is named. He had received his advanced degree at Harvard and had studied with such eminent scientists as Asa Gray in biology and Louis Agasiz in geology. After the Civil War, he had worked with the Baltimore Association of Friends in reconstuction work in North Carolina. From 1868 until 1883 he had been Earlham's distinguished President. Then he resigned to spend two years raising funds to put Earlham on a better financial footing. Following that he served as principal of the New Garden Boarding School in North Carolina during the period when it was becoming Guilford College. Now he was back in Earlham, teaching science and working diligently on his beloved science collection, which was later to become the Joseph Moore Museum.

David Worth Dennis was another extremely able member of the faculty; he served thirty-two years as a science professor. To perpetuate his contributions to the college and to honor him, the present science building bears his name. He was also the father of William Cullen Dennis, the president of Earlham from 1929 until 1946.

In 1888 Edwin P. Trueblood came to Earlham as Governor of Boys, as a speech teacher, and as an athletic instructor. It was "Prof. Ed," as he was later known affectionately by generations of Earlhamites, who launched the speech department at Earlham. His brother, Thomas Clarkson Trueblood, was doing the same at the University of Michigan. These were the first two departments of that kind in the United States. For fifty years (from 1888 until 1838) Professor Trueblood remained at Earlham. Another famous Earlham professor was William N. Trueblood, a Shakespeare scholar and an inspiring teacher of literature; he served on the faculty for forty-five years.

An eccentric, but much beloved, professor at that time was Adolph Gerber. Murray did not study with him, but the college was small enough that Gerber was well known to all the students. Many were the stories which Murray and Violet Kenworthy told throughout their lives about the oddities of that teacher of German.

These and other members of the faculty were unusual persons. Exposure to them and their thinking was a great stimulus to the New London farm boy who spent four years at Earlham College in the 1890s.

Murray Kenworthy knew well why he was at Earlham College, especially as he had to work hard to pay for his education. He studied hard and was a good student. In fact he was so good as a student and so engaging as a personality that he attracted the attention of Elbert Russell, the head of the Biblical Department, who later invited him back to Earlham as his assistant.

Murray also realized the importance of extra or co-curricular activities and the fun and education they provided. Consequently he took an active part in several of them. In his freshman year, in 1893-1984, he was chosen as president of his class, a high honor.

Intercollegiate athletics were relatively new at that time and Murray was on the Earlham College football team. *The Earlhamite* for that year reported that the college had had its best season in its history in contests with DePauw, Miami, Rose Polytechnic, Purdue, and Wittenberg. It was in the Purdue game that Murray scored the only touchdown that Earlham ever had against that state school, later too large for Earlham to play it. He also took part in field and track events, becoming outstanding as a sprinter.

Probably Murray took part in oratorical contests, but there is no record of them. There are however, accounts of his role as an intercollegiate debater, an activity which had become a major "sport" on many college campuses in those days, spurred on by the first intercollegiate debate between Harvard and Yale in 1892. In the May 5, 1900, issue of *The Earlhamite* the lead story was about the Earlham College–Indiana University debate in which Earlham's team took the affirmative side on the topic: Resolved that the regular army of the United States be maintained at its present strength of sixty-five thousand men.

The Earlham team traveled to DePauw and stayed there overnight, proceeding then to Bloomington. Before the debate there the students spent a half-hour singing songs and giving yells to spur on their team. It sounds unbelievable now, but it was not unbelievable then.

When the news of the Earlham victory was received in Richmond, *The Earlhamite* reported that:

> At 10:45 when the ringing of the college bell with the various-pitched voices keyed to every conceivable pitch which the human voice can produce...announced victory had been scored, every available instrument for jollification augmented the glad news....Pandemonium reigned....The tell-tale bonfire flared up (and) an Indian war-dance kept time to the crackling pine boxes and the "Keep Off The Grass" signs.

It said further that the crowd then set off to the President's house to celebrate there. On the following Saturday there was a reception for the debaters after dinner, complete with an informal program. Such was the high priority placed on debating at the time.

Murray was also active in the Young Men's Christian Association and often preached in the Friends meetings in Richmond and in nearby small towns. In his senior year he was president of the Ionian Literary Society, a club for men (with a corresponding group for women). One of its major activities (in conjunction with the alumni) was the production of *The Earlhamite*, the first college alumni paper in the United States. Murray was also a member of the History Club, occasionally presenting a paper or giving a talk in that group.

In his senior year Murray took a course in surveying, largely because he had been nominated for the office of surveyor in Howard County. Probably that was on the Prohibition Party ticket; he would surely have been elected if he had been the Republican candidate in that part of Indiana around the turn of the century.

With his graduation in 1900 Murray Kenworthy was ready to enter the public ministry of the Religious Society of Friends as one of its most able and best-educated young leaders. What a remarkable contribution those four years at Earlham had made to him, and through him, to others. How much his world had widened.

Despite his full schedule of classes and his various extracurricular activities, he must have had some time for the limited social life permitted at Earlham in those days. He and Ida Lenora Holloway became close friends. Lenora was a graduate of the Spiceland Academy and a classmate of Murray's when they graduated from Earlham in 1900. In September, 1902, they were married.

Lenora Holloway Kenworthy (the name she used after her marriage) was the daughter of Asa Holloway, a very successful farmer. He was active in the Friends meeting of Spiceland, Indiana, a predominantly Quaker community where the Holloways lived all their life.

Lenora's mother taught school in Indiana and then went south with her sister after the Civil War to organize schools for Negroes, under the auspices of the Indiana Yearly Meeting Freedmen's Association. After the birth of Lenora and her brother, Arthur, "Lizzie" Edwards Holloway went to Chicago and studied medicine at the Hahnemann Hospital (specializing in homeopathic practices). She became one of the first women doctors in the Midwest. She played the organ, served many years as a trustee of the Spiceland (Friends) Academy, and was writing a paper on the League of Nations and the World Court when she died in 1927 at the age of 93.

Lenora was an attractive young woman, slim in build, with a dark complexion, and long, jet black hair. She was a talented singer and she played the piano well.

As a girl Lenora had had rheumatic fever and as a young woman she suffered at times from inflammatory rheumatism and frequent headaches, probably as a result of her illness as a child. She was a woman of high standards and possessed all the social graces. She was a wonderful wife and helpmate to Murray, a dedicated mother to her three sons, and a steady influence in the Friends meetings and communities in which she and Murray eventually worked.

TEACHING AT EARLHAM COLLEGE

In his early teens Murray Kenworthy spoke from time to time in the "open period" of the Friends Meeting at New London. During that period of his life he became clear that he was called to the public ministry of Friends. In his notes on his life he commented that at the age of eighteen "I attempted in the early winter my first prepared sermon at Bethel" (a Quaker meeting near New London).

That sense of Divine direction in his life led him to Earlham and to courses there in the Biblical Department, with some public ministry while he was still a student. After graduation, he preached for a summer at the Section, near Azalia, and for three months in Muncie, during the absence of the pastor there because of a serious illness. From 1900 to 1902 he was the pastor of the Paoli Friends Meeting in southern Indiana, a community with many of his relatives on the Stout side of the family.

In 1902 he moved with his bride, Lenora Holloway Kenworthy, to Kokomo, the county seat of Howard County, in which he had been born and brought up, to serve the Friends meeting there as its pastor. Meanwhile he continued his studies at Earlham as best he could, earning his master's degree in 1905.

At that time we assume that Elbert Russell had been keeping his eyes on this gifted and promising young Quaker. When the Biblical Department grew, Elbert asked that Murray Kenworthy be added to the faculty of Earlham College. His qualifications for that post were numerous: he was a Hoosier with a solid Quaker background, a graduate of Earlham, a former student of Elbert Russell (with whom he shared his views on most matters), and a person with a few years' experience in several Friends meetings. He was three years younger than Elbert Russell and had a little lighter touch which would enhance the effectiveness of the department. Furthermore, they were both of an age to start their families and to be close friends, good neighbors, and outstanding citizens of Richmond.

The appointment was an ideal one for all the parties concerned, and President Robert L. Kelly concurred with it. Therefore Murray and Lenora moved back to Richmond where they were to spend a long period of their lives (1904 until 1915). Two of those years involved a leave-of-absence in Massachusetts where Murray studied at Harvard Divinity School.

Since Murray's graduation in 1900, Richmond had grown in population and changed in numerous ways. In 1818 it had had two hundred residents, in 1850, almost four thousand. Now it had around twenty thousand. Horseless carriages or gas buggies were on the streets. At one time Richmond was the locale for producing fourteen different automobiles—the earliest being the Wayne, Richmond, Pilot, Davis, and Wescott. In 1905 Reid Memorial Hospital was built on land donated by Daniel Reid as a memorial to his wife and son. New industries had been started as the Garr, Scott, and Company (manufacturers of threshers and traction and portable engines), the Robinson Manufacturing Company (later the Swayne Robinson Company), and the Starr Piano Company.

Richmond was large enough to accommodate a variety of people, churches, schools, factories, and stores, yet small enough to encourage friendly interchanges and a chance for people to have a direct influence on it as citizens.

Richmond was a pleasant place to live, work, and raise a family. Murray and Lenora purchased four lots from Elbert and Lieuetta Russell, next door to them, on the National Road West, and started to built a simple but comfortable frame house—known for a few years as the Kenworthy home and for succeeding generations as the Millard Markle residence. Murray did a great deal of the construction of that house cutting some of the costs and giving him a chance to use his skills as a carpenter, plumber, and electrician.

Carroll Kenworthy had been born in Kokomo in 1904. Now Wilmer and Leonard were born in the new Kenworthy home in 1908 and in 1912, respectively. Murray and Lenora must have thought they would stay there for the rest of their lives. It was a congenial community; the college teaching and preaching met Murray's two interests. It was an ideal place to raise children–especially with the college campus as almost their front yard and good neighbors like the Russells, the Holes, the Nicholsons, and others.

There had been changes at the college since the days when Murray and Lenora were students, especially with the shift of the presidency in 1903 from Joseph John Mills to Robert L. Kelly.

Kelly had graduated from Earlham, served as an administrator in the public schools of Monrovia, Indiana, at the Raisin Valley Seminary (a Friends School in Adrian, Michigan), and at the rapidly expanding Central (Friends) Academy in Plainfield, Indiana, before becoming Earlham's new head. He had taken graduate work at the University of Chicago in philosophy and psychology and served as Acting President of Penn College in Oskaloosa, Iowa. He combined scholarship, a Quaker outlook, and a firm hand on the reins of administration; his opponents said too firm a hand. In 1900 the Preparatory Department was closed because of the growth of public high schools in Indiana, and under President Kelly the graduates of the Quaker academies were no longer given the status of sophomores upon entrance to Earlham. This raised the academic level in the eyes of most college administrators.

Several of the faculty under whom Murray had studied were still there. Others, with equally high credentials, had been added. New departments were being created and an enlarged faculty hired. Dramatics was added to the Speech Department; art and music were upgraded.

To take care of the expanding student body, Bundy Hall was built in 1907 as the men's residence and a library was built with funds raised to match an initial grant of thirty thousand dollars from Andrew Carnegie. Furthermore, the endowment, still pitifully small, was increased considerably.

All those changes had not yet occurred when Murray Kenworthy returned to Earlham as a faculty member, but they did take place in a few years under the administration of President Kelly. Thus it became a stronger institution than it had been when Murray was a student.

As has already been noted, Murray Kenworthy went to Earlham to assist Elbert Russell who had been the only member of the Biblical Department until that time. Elbert Russell was born in 1871 in Friendsville, Tennessee, and lived there for the first seven years of his life. As a boy the major influence on him was his father–a graduate of Earlham College, a recorded minister, a farmer and teacher, and for six years the principal of the Friendsville Academy, a Quaker institution. Elbert's father was a voracious reader, an amateur poet, a peace advocate (having opposed the Civil War), and an ardent prohibitionist. According to his son, he also had "a rather sceptical attitude toward popular beliefs and superstitions."

Both of Elbert's parents died when he was seven, and so he and his sister went to live with their Russell grandparents in Valley Mills, Indiana, near Indianapolis. When he graduated from the local high school, Elbert read an essay on George Fox–a forerunner of his work as a Quaker historian.

In college days at Earlham, he became a member of the staff of *The Earlhamite,* president of the YMCA, and the winner of third place in the state oratorical contest. Although shaken profoundly by his chance reading of a book by the "arch-infidel"–Robert Ingersoll, he had recovered from the original shock to his easily-held beliefs and begun to work out a more tenable religious faith, aided by his contacts with several leading YMCA leaders, including the famous John R. Mott, whom he had met at a YMCA conference at Lake Geneva, Wisconsin.

In 1894-1895 there had been an upheaval at Earlham because of the identification of Dougan Clark of the Biblical Department with the extreme wing of Quakers, led by David Updegraff, when that small group defended the practice of water baptism and the celebration of the Lord's Supper by Friends. Clark had been released from his post at Earlham, and President Kelly had asked Elbert Russell to take his place.

Elbert had almost no training in theology or Quaker history, but that seemed like a plus to Kelly and those who were skeptical about advanced work in such fields by Quakers. So, even though Elbert was working on his master's degree in foreign languages at Earlham, he was appointed. That was in 1895. He studied hard and read widely and was popular with his students, but he was aware of how poor his preparation had been. Eventually he obtained a leave of absence to study at the University of Chicago Divinity School from 1900 to 1903. There he had work with President Harper, Dean Shailer Matthew, Edgar J. Goodspeed (the translator of the New Testament into a version bearing his name), and others.

Elbert Russell returned to Earlham thoroughly grounded in the work he would resume, and, according to his own comment, he "did not cease to be a rather idealistic progressive, but...did not become a destructive radical." He was basically a scholar, but he realized that it was important "to be interesting as well as intelligent." So he worked on that, too.

In the first decade of the twentieth century Elbert Russell taught at several Bible Institutes at Earlham in the summer and went east to attend one of the famous summer schools at Haverford College, where he met such prominent Quakers as Rufus Jones of Haverford and J. Rendel Harris and John Wilhelm Rowntree of England. Elbert also served as the Quaker representative on a committee of the Historic Peace Churches (the Brethren, the Mennonites, and the Quakers). Soon he was in demand as a speaker at various yearly meetings in the Midwest, East, and South.

Murray had studied under Elbert Russell as a student at Earlham; now he returned to teach with him in the Biblical Department. In those days that department had many students in it–479 between 1896 and 1906. In the year 1906-1907 there were thirty-four ministers, prospective ministers, and missionaries studying in it. Elbert Russell specialized in the Old Testament and Murray Kenworthy in the New Testament. Each of them conducted many of the college chapel programs, and they shared the responsibility for the preaching at the Friends Meeting held at the college on Sundays.

In addition, Murray preached for several months at Selma and Ludlow Falls, Ohio, and served as pastor of the recently-organized Quaker group in Dayton, Ohio. During another year he served as the Earlham representative to the quarterly meetings, trying to foster friendly relationships between the college and its basic constituencies–Western and Indiana Yearly Meeting. Then, between 1911 and 1915, he was the first pastor of the newly organized West Richmond Friends Meeting.

During this time theological differences were much in evidence among Friends and these differences vitally affected Murray's life. Toward the end of the nineteenth century and in the beginning of the twentieth, two forces were at work in the Religious Society of Friends in the United States. One was a trend toward unity, or at least, cooperation. The other was a split among American Quakers between conservatives or fundamentalists and liberals or modernists. Centrifugal and centripetal forces were operating simultaneously.

As a result of a series of conferences over a period of several years, most of the Orthodox yearly meetings formed the Five Years Meeting in 1902, with headquarters in Richmond. At the same time the Hicksite yearly meetings formed a more flexible federation, known as Friends General Conference, with headquarters in Philadelphia. Meanwhile the winds of theological controversy had been blowing, especially in the midwest, and sometimes they reached hurricane proportions, doing damage to individuals, meetings, institutions, and the Society of Friends as a whole.

During the period when many midwestern meetings were hiring

pastors and becoming programmed or semi-programmed in their worship services, it was the elders who were most often opposed to those changes. When the innovations finally were instituted, the elders were frequently replaced by the pastors as the most influential or weighty Friends. That was especially noticeable in committee appointments at the quarterly and yearly meeting levels. One added factor which helps to explain the increasing role of pastors in the affairs of Quaker groups was the fact that they often had more time which could be devoted to such matters than other members had.

There is no doubt of the devotion of nearly all of those new pastors. They certainly worked unceasingly in the Lord's vineyard–and at pitiful salaries. By and large, however, they were extremely conservative theologically. Most of them had been farmers and had little education. Few of them had had opportunities to travel or work outside a narrow geographical area. Many of them were from other denominations, and they brought their religious beliefs with them, often with only a veneer of Quakerism added. For the most part, they believed in revival meetings and other evangelistic practices. In fact, many of them had been evangelists before they became pastors.

Confronted with challenges to their conservative beliefs by such ideas as evolution, higher criticism of the Bible, and the call for the social gospel, they condemned those modern views and those who held them. Those conservative pastors and their supporters felt that they were upholding the historic views of Christianity and of Quakerism; they could cite chapters and verses from the Bible and from the writings of George Fox and Robert Barclay to uphold their views.

There were other Friends in that period, however, who were adherents, at least in part, of the new views of contemporary Christianity and of twentieth century Quakerism. They tended to be men and women who had traveled more widely, read more, studied in institutions of higher learning, and could accept new views without destroying their faith. In many ways those new views freed them to reassess and reshape their faith and thus deepen, extend, and heighten it. They felt that thereby they were not less Christian or less Quakerly, but more so.

Of course there were many positions on the continuum of religious beliefs, then, as now. But for our purposes here, let us oversimplify them by calling one group the sin, salvation, and sanctification faction as opposed to the spiritually-minded and socially-conscious faction, or Party A and Party B.

More specifically, Party A stressed the historic Christ and believed in him as their Lord and Savior. They believed that by his death on the cross he had purchased the salvation of men and women who came after him. Most of them believed literally in the Second Coming. To them Heaven and Hell were actual places and the Devil, a person, the counterpart to God. They believed in human depravity, and preaching against sin loomed large in their ministry. The Creation took place, according to them, in six days of twenty-four hours each, and creation then ceased. Revelation came to prophets and to Jesus but was rare, if at all possible, later. Rigidly or faithfully, according to one's interpretation, they held to a long list of sins which constituted pretty much their social concern. To them the chief aim in life was to be saved and to prepare for the next world. The Bible was the absolute Word of God, inspired if not even dictated by God, and it was the final authority in matters theological, spiritual, and even social. In methodology they believed strongly in revival meetings and other evangelistic methods. Many names were given to that group, conservatives or fundamentalists being the most common titles.

In Party B there was a wider range of beliefs or attitudes,–so much flexibility according to their opponents that they said members of that group could believe anything–or nothing. The contention of adherents of Party B was that there are many paths to Truth and to God. By and large the members of the modernist group stressed the historic Christ *and* the contemporary or continuing Christ. In theology they were still trinitarians, not humanists. Although the cross meant much to them, they felt that men and women earned their own salvation by leading Christian lives rather than by some transaction between God and Jesus. Rather than the literal return of Christ in the flesh, they agreed with Fox that "Christ is come" to judge his people, stressing the importance of the verb in the present tense. Rather than human beings being born in sin, they contended that God so loved the world and human beings that he equipped every person with something of the divine in all those who entered this earth. That Divinity could be ignored or by-passed but it was always there, and in everyone, ready to be developed. Human beings were therefore "a little lower than the angels...and clothed in glory and honor." Thus the modernists were positivists rather than negativists.

Furthermore, the modernists or liberals believed that the Creation had taken place over a period of eons but was nevertheless a God-given process. And to them the creation continued; some even asserting that God grows. Returning to the beliefs of early Christians and early Quakers, they emphasized continuing revelation, saying that the day of the saints and the prophets was not over. To them Heaven and Hell were probably not actual places and the Devil more likely to be a force in the lives of human beings than an actual person.

To them the Bible was inspiring and parts of it probably inspired. But it was not infallible, and they pointed out its many contradictions. To them it was a source of authority but secondary to the primary authority of direct revelation—God speaking to men, women, and children.

Elbert Russell and Murray Kenworthy found it difficult to characterize sin easily or glibly, but they believed that there were "sins." Those included social, economic, educational, and political sins as well as personal ones. They took literally the part of the Lord's Prayer which called for all human beings to strive for the creation of God's Kingdom "on earth as it is in heaven." Thus their emphasis was upon the here rather than upon the hereafter. Different names were applied to the proponents of these beliefs. Usually they were called liberals or modernists.

Again, neither of the descriptions recorded above would represent a single individual's view. In the aggregate, however, they represent to me the two dominant ideas of many Christians and of many Quakers in the first few years of this century—and even today.

In light of these theological differences, one can see why Elbert Russell and Murray Kenworthy soon became the targets for those opposed to the views of liberals or modernists. Both men were highly educated. Both were graduates of divinity schools and had studied with some of the great biblical scholars of their time. Both had travelled widely and lived in a variety of places. Thus their experiential background was broad. Furthermore both of them were excellent speakers and good organizers. They had attractive personalities and were both likely to have a tremendous influence on the young people at Earlham College and elsewhere.

It was therefore not surprising that those who felt that Russell and Kenworthy had pernicious theological views should feel that they were subverting a whole generation of future Quaker leaders and changing the course of the mainstream of Quakerism, especially in the Midwest. They were. The witch-hunt began slowly at first, subtly, then more openly and more pronounced. Statements were circulated that they were living in luxury, that their children were hoodlums and were being raised in Godless homes; that those men did not really believe in God and admitted that the Bible was not sacred. They might not even believe in the Virgin Birth, the Second Coming, or other basic Christian and Quaker tenets.

A few students kept notes on what Elbert Russell and Murray Kenworthy said in their classes, in chapel talks, or in their sermons on Sundays—with misquotes or quotes out of context. By that time Elbert

36

Russell was being asked to speak at conferences and various yearly meetings. Not one to mince words, he said what he thought and let others decide whether he was misleading a generation of young Quakers. He even invited leading opponents to come to his classes and stay in his home to see for themselves what he was propounding and how he was raising his family.

There is little to be gained by a blow-by-blow description of what happened to those two Quakers over a period of several years. Suffice it to say that they were criticized, censured, and condemned by some and championed by others, especially recent graduates who had studied with them. However, Russell and Kenworthy were primarily symbols of a much wider struggle between fundamentalists and modernists in the Religious Society of Friends and in the wider world.

It is relevant to add that in the case of Elbert Russell there were other forces at work to oust him from Earlham. One was the fact that he had a dream of a meetinghouse on the campus which would serve the Earlham students, the growing group of Friends in West Richmond, Indiana Yearly Meeting at its annual sessions, and, less frequently, the nation-wide body of Friends who were a part of the Five Years Meeting of Friends. East Main Street Friends had just enlarged their meeting-house, however, and were unalterably opposed to the plan for a large structure on the Earlham campus. The other two factors were Russell's criticism of William O. Mendenhall, a young professor who was in charge of the men and whom Russell felt was "lax" in his administration. Russell also felt that Mendenhall was meddling in the Earlham YMCA, which was Russell's responsibility. In that conflict President Kelly supported Mendenhall and that irked Elbert Russell.

When the plan for a meetinghouse on the Earlham campus failed, West Richmond friends decided to build their own structure near the campus on West Main Street. Murray was their first pastor, although he continued his teaching at the college.

Murray's work in that Friends meeting was especially successful with an unusual group of young people, many of whom later became prominent in Quaker organizations and movements. That group included Juanita Ballard, Paul and Dorothy Heironimus, William McMinn, Caroline and Francis Nicholson, Charles Robinson, Josiah and Marcia Russell, and others.

In all of the tension created by the various situations at Earlham, Murray Kenworthy became a pawn in the giant chess game between the fundamentalists and the modernists. The strategy of the fundamentalists was to test their strength in getting rid of Kenworthy. Then, if they succeeded, they would try to remove Elbert Russell.

Their plan worked, and in 1915 Murray Kenworthy resigned and returned to the Harvard Divinity School. Within a few years Elbert Russell was also forced to resign. Eventually Professor Mendenhall and President Kelly also left.

In her history of Earlham Opal Thornburg comments:

> So the affair, perhaps the saddest of Earlham's history, came officially to a conclusion....

It says much for the men involved and for the college that all four of them went on to positions of leadership elsewhere and still all of them remained loyal to Earlham.

AT HARVARD DIVINITY SCHOOL

Although Elbert Russell had taken his graduate work at the University of Chicago, he apparently urged Murray Kenworthy to do his advanced study at the Harvard Divinity School. That was probably in part due to the fact that Walter Rauschenbusch was a professor there. It also may be that a contributing factor was the fact that Murray could preach in nearby Friends meetings–first in Lynn and at a later time in Fall River, Massachusetts.

Murray went to Harvard for the period from 1909 to 1911 and returned for the academic year of 1915-1916 to earn the S.T.B. (Bachelor of Sacred Theology) degree, equivalent then to a Doctor of Divinity Degree. During the first period of study the four Kenworthys lived in Lynn, and in the second period the five Kenworthys lived in Cambridge.

Murray was extremely busy, but he did find time now and then to see the sights of that Cradle of Liberty and to take the older boys with him to visit Lexington and Concord, Fanueil Hall, the Old North Church, the Boston Common, and other places in Boston and in its environs.

Probably he was the first midwestern Quaker to study at the Harvard Divinity School. Also there was Henry J. Cadbury, a Philadelphia Quaker and a graduate of Haverford College who became famous later as a Quaker historian, the chairman for many years of the American Friends Service Committee, and one of the scholars who translated the New Testament in the revised version.

It is curious that these two Quakers were there at the same time. In at least one class they sat together. Murray commented later in life that he enjoyed that immensely because Henry's notes were often better than the lectures!

Not only were the winds of change blowing in theology; they were blowing in such fields as education, psychology, and philosophy. John Dewey was opening new vistas in philosophy and in education with his emphasis upon direct experience and the involvement of pupils as the basis of true learning. In psychology, philosophy, and education, William James was heralding a new day with the publication of such books as *The Principles of Psychology, The Will to Believe,* and *The Varieties of Religious Experience.*

And in sociology, economics, and politics, Ida Tarbell was exposing the machinations of "the robber barons" in her *History of the Standard Oil Company;* Lincoln Steffens was revealing the corruption in municipal politics in *The Shame of Cities;* Jacob Riis was disturbing the complacency of upper and middle-class Americans through his book, *How the Other Half Lives,* which depicted the poverty and squalor of life in large American cities.

Even more earth-shaking was the doctrine of evolution propounded principally by Charles Darwin in his *Origin of the Species, The Descent of Man,* and other writings. Although written earlier in the nineteenth century, Darwin's ideas were just beginning to wrack the religious community in the United States of America.

For those who believed in the literal interpretation of the Bible, Darwin's ideas were shattering. If accepted, they would destroy the foundation of their faith–that God had actually created the world in six days of twenty–four hours each and that the Bible had been dictated by the Divine. Challenged by the "heresies" of Darwin and others, they launched a counter-offensive, one which is still going on. But it was even more bitter in the years around 1900 than it is today.

Other religious leaders, however, took a very different view. To them God was still the Creator, whether the six days were composed of twenty-four hours each or of eons of time. To them creation continued; even God could change and grow. To them the Bible was a record of people's struggles to understand the Divine and a growing grasp of the greatness of God and the potential grandeur of humans. They agreed that God had revealed Himself to people in former times, but they felt that God was still revealing Himself to human beings; revelation continued.

Those religious leaders counselled cooperation between scientists and religionists rather than championing confrontation and conflict.

Coupled with those beliefs was the conviction of modernists that Christians should be far more concerned with the here than with the hereafter. They took literally the call of Jesus in the Lord's Prayer that God's will should be done on earth as in heaven.

The leading proponent of those views was Walter Rauschenbush, a professor at the Harvard Divinity School. In 1907 his volume on *Christianity and the Social Crisis* appeared, sending shock waves through a large segment of American Christendom. Rauschenbusch's passion for social justice had been developed in part by his reading and study of the Bible, and in part by eleven years as pastor of a congregation of working people in the west side of New York City. The book just referred to was written as a partial debt to those people whose lot was not a happy one.

Christianity and the Social Crisis was a powerful document. In it he maintained that five centuries of recent revolutions had resulted in a social crisis for the current generation. Although slow in coming to this hemisphere, it was now causing an upheaval and a realignment in thinking and in action. "We are," he said, "today in the midst of a revolutionary epoch fully as thorough as that of the Renaissance and the Reformation."

In that crisis, he asserted, the Church should not stand on the sidelines because:

> ...the essential purpose of Christianity (is) to transform human society into the Kingdom of God by regenerating human relations and reconstructing them in accordance with the will of God.

He pointed out that throughout history "minority men" had tried to move the masses and the rulers by speaking truth to power, even though those truths were often unpopular. He called such individuals "heralds of the fundamental truth that religion and ethics are inseparable." Among such heralds were Amos, Hosea, Jeremiah, Micah, and the other Old Testament prophets. They were champions of the poor and the oppressed, defenders of justice, social reformers.

To Rauschenbusch the life and teachings of Jesus revealed "a revolutionary consciousness," "the inauguration of a new humanity." In a typical passage he wrote:

> Jesus, like the prophets and like all his spiritually-minded

countrymen, lived in the hope of a great transformation of the
national, social, and religious life about Him.

To him beliefs were important, but actions even more important.

Referring to the talk that Jesus had with the rich young man,
Rauschenbush pointed out that he expressed the view in that
conversation that "riches were the most divisive element in any
society." Rauschenbush believed that Jesus had the scientific insight
which comes to most men only by training, but to the elect by divine
gift.

Turning to the early Church, he claimed that it united two important
streams of thought. From its Hebrew origin it brought the social hope;
from its Greek environment it accepted the intensification of the
individual hope.

According to that Harvard Divinity School professor, Jesus eschewed
violence, rejecting the powers he could have summoned to accomplish
his purposes. Unfortunately, as is true in so many revolutionary
movements, the dream faded. The small, intimate, sharing fellowships
became large, rigid, ritualistic, authoritarian organizations. Thus the
hopeful, radical minority became the comfortable and sometimes
oppressive majority.

Rauschenbush called for a return to first-century Christianity to
reclaim the vision of personal redemption coupled with social
revolution to bring about a better society. To him:

> All human goodness must be social goodness....A man is
> moral when he is social; he is immoral when he is anti-
> social....The highest type of goodness is that which puts
> freely at the service of the community all that a man is and can
> (do)....

He desired the replacement of a ritual-centered Christianity with a
socially-active Christianity. God was too small and too far away as
interpreted by so many Christians of his day. Cogently and
persuasively, and in highly quotable language, he pled for individual *and*
social salvation. He lamented the fact that the Christian Church had
never really undertaken such a dual purpose.

Such views were not completely new to Murray Kenworthy. He had
heard them espoused by his mentor and friend, Elbert Russell, and by a
few others. And they rang true to what he knew about George Fox and
the early Friends. But they came now with new authority and with a
fresh challenge from someone he admired.

All the professors with whom he studied taught him much, but it was Walter Rauschenbusch who affected him most deeply. He broadened Murray's background in the Bible, altered his view of Jesus, and fortified and extended his belief in the importance of social action based on religious convictions. At least as much as Elbert Russell, probably even more so, Rauschenbusch widened Murray's world in a theological and in a sociological sense.

SERVING GLEN FALLS AND WILMINGTON QUAKERS

Completing his work at the Harvard Divinity School, Murray Kenworthy moved his family to Glens Falls, New York, where he became pastor of the Friends meeting there. Glens Falls was an attractive town of around fifteen thousand persons, located at the falls of the Hudson River and close to the Adirondack Mountains. It was near limestone and black marble quarries and had several paper mills and cement, brick, and chemical plants. However, its major claim to prominence came from two sources. One was Cooper's Cave, at the foot of the falls, named for James Fennimore Cooper, who had immortalized that setting in an episode in *The Last of the Mohicans*. The other was the local insurance company which achieved national attention when it paid its customers promptly and in full when they lost property in the disastrous earthquake of 1906 in San Francisco.

No one seems to know why Murray decided to move there. Possibly it was because he was not in great demand in the Midwest after the Earlham episode. His further work at Harvard may have made him even more formidable to some people and more suspect to others as a young radical. It seems likely that Friends in Glens Falls were more liberal and glad to attract a young man with the breadth of experiences, the depth of scholarship, the spiritual maturity, and the native abilities which he had. In any case, the Kenworthys moved there in 1916 and remained until 1919.

In those days the Glens Falls Meeting was a thriving one. It was housed in a large, red-brick building with ample Sunday School rooms and an auditorium which was large enough to hold the sessions of New York Yearly Meeting (Orthodox) which sometimes convened there. Attendance at Sunday School was around two hundred and at the Sunday meeting for worship, 150. There were several prominent Quaker families in that group, including the Careys, the Eddys, the Sellecks, and the Varneys. And there were a few Quaker farmers in the area around Glens Falls.

Just behind the meetinghouse, at 37 Grand Street, was the comfortable parsonage. It was big enough to house the five Kenworthys and Grandmother Holloway when she came to spend the winters there, and for Murray to have a room for his study, heated from the kitchen stove below.

Some ministers are good preachers and some good pastors. Murray Kenworthy was both. He developed a routine which made those two complementary aspects of his work outstanding. In the morning he would retire to his study to work on his sermon, to plan and/or carry out various meeting projects, and to work on his correspondence. Then, in the afternoons, he called on members and attenders, an aspect of his work for which he became well-known in all of his pastorates. He made those visits largely on foot and must have walked hundreds of miles during those three years in Glens Falls.

The meeting included a large and active group of young people, and he reveled in the work with them as he had done in West Richmond. He attended almost all their meetings, and he and Lenora planned many social events for that group, several of them in the parsonage. One of the leading members of that Young Friends group was LeRoy De-Marsh, who later became a well-known Quaker minister and pastor. Others took leading roles in the Glens Falls Meeting and in New York Yearly Meeting as they became older.

On Saturdays Murray often took his three sons on walks or to interesting places in the vicinity, such as the paper mill with its great vats of pulp which were turned into huge rolls of paper. Occasionally there were longer and more difficult jaunts with Carroll and Wilmer. They would take the trolley with their father as far as it went and then start hiking in the foothills of the Adirondacks. In the fall they gathered chestnuts and brought them home to roast, reminiscent for Murray of his boyhood in Indiana.

Lenora was an outstanding cook, and I still recall some of her favorite dishes. One was a Saturday night repast which she had learned to prepare in New England–Boston baked beans with brown bread–filled with raisins, and baked in tin cans. Another was her New England dinner, replete with some meat, potatoes, carrots, cabbage, and onions, all prepared in one large receptacle. Then there was the "floating island" pudding, lemon pies, and a fruit salad filled with diced marshmallows and topped with shredded coconut. Glens Falls was near the famous apple district of New York state, so there were barrels of them in the winter, kept fresh in sawdust.

The winters were cold; many nights the temperature would go to twenty degrees below zero and one night it went to forty degrees below that special spot. All the Kenworthys remember the snow beside the meetinghouse which was packed almost like ice and remained there until May or even into June.

Carroll entered the eighth grade in the Glens Falls public schools but not without some difficulty. When he was taken to school by his father, the principal said that Carroll should be assigned to the seventh grade because his preparation in Cambridge would not have prepared him for the rigorous program of the Glens Falls schools. Murray Kenworthy seldom intervened in such matters, but that time he did. He pointed out that the children of Harvard University professors and graduate students attended the schools in Cambridge and the instruction in their institutions was every bit as good as it was in Glens Falls. That fall and winter Carroll put an extra effort into his studies, with more than the usual amount of help from his father. But their efforts paid off. Because of World War I, the boys with superior grades were allowed to leave school early in the spring to help farmers. So, with his good grades, Carroll was furloughed to Indiana to help his Grandfather Kenworthy.

That fall Carroll entered Oakwood School, the New York Yearly Meeting secondary institution in Union Springs, New York, on the shores of one of the Finger Lakes, Lake Cayuga. The principal at that time was William Reagan whom Murray had known ever since their days in New London, Indiana. Murray thought he was an outstanding principal, and he also knew that the school needed all the students and support it could get to survive. It was in Carroll's senior year that Oakwood School moved back to the Poughkeepsie, New York, area where it had been started and where it still remains.

One summer Lenora and Leonard took the train to Indiana to visit the Holloway relatives in Spiceland, Indiana, while Murray and the two older boys went to North Carolina. Murray had been invited to speak at the session of North Carolina Yearly Meeting and felt it would be good for him to spend some time with Carroll and Wilmer on that automobile journey.

Once those meetings were over, they set out for Indiana, traveling through some hazardous areas of North Carolina, Tennessee, and Kentucky. It was a memorable trip for all three of them. Flat tires were frequent in those days, and time had to be taken to vulcanize the inner tubes. In many places they discovered that the roads were not much more than cow paths or the beds of streams. For example, in one stretch of thirteen miles they crossed the same stream eight times and drove for rods along the bed. Frequently Murray would stop the car, get out, and measure the height of the stumps to see if the automobile could pass over the without breaking some part. Usually they succeeded, but one time they failed. To their dismay they realized that the "wishbone" of the car had been broken and that there was nothing to do but have Murray leave his sons and set out on foot for the nearest garage. It proved to be eight miles away. But he was lucky that it had the needed part. Then he had to trudge back all those miles and attach the new part before they could resume their trip.

Eventually they arrived in Indiana, tired and dirty. Murray had grown a full beard in the interval since they had left North Carolina. They were welcomed by the Holloway and Edwards relatives and given a special treat of watermelons and muskmelons from their Uncle David Edwards' garden. Over on the sidelines was Leonard, a bit frightened by the appearance of someone they said was his father.

When Murray went to Glens Falls, World War I had already been going on for two years. The United States had kept out of that dreadful conflagration despite its sympathy for the Allies. But the ties of culture, tradition, and common institutions, the economic involvement of the United States of America, the unrestricted submarine warfare, the alleged atrocities against the Belgians, and other factors caused the entrance of the United States against the Central Powers and war was declared against them by the U.S.A. on Good Friday, April 6, 1917.

Few people today can imagine how bitter the feeling in the United States was against the Germans and their allies. Little incidents may indicate how far that bitterness extended. German songs were torn out of songbooks and hymnals. Places like Germantown, Indiana, changed their names—in that case to Pershing. Sauerkraut was renamed Victory Cabbage and hamburgers became Liberty Steak.

As a pacifist the war posed some problems for Murray. He was forthright about his views, based on his interpretation of the life and teachings of Jesus, but he did not flaunt them. Nevertheless his pacifism was well known. Most members of the Friends meeting respected him for his opinions, although they did not all share them. For example, one member wanted to purchase a Liberty Bond in Murray's name, to show his "loyalty," an offer he declined. In the wider community he was often criticized. Even some of his ministerial colleagues and friends would deliberately cross the street if they saw him coming, in order to avoid having to speak to him.

Meanwhile, some young Quakers in various parts of the United States stood by the historical peace testimony of Friends and refused to take part in the war. There was no alternative service in World War I, and objectors frequently suffered for their beliefs. A few were lined up, facing lines of fixed bayonets and guns, in the hope that they would recant when faced with death. Other had their faces stuck in latrines for long periods in order to force them to take part in the war.

Fortunately, the newly formed American Friends Service Committee was able to persuade the United States government to set up a camp for conscientious objectors. It was located near Kennett Square, Pennsylvania. Murray was asked by Vincent Nicholson, the executive secretary of the AFSC, to head that camp. How interesting that Vincent was the son of S. Edgar Nicholson, the high school principal in New London, Indiana, who had urged Murray to go to Earlham.

The Glens Falls Meeting released Murray to go to Haverford College when C.O.s were sent there from army bases before going to the Rosedale Farm near Kennett Square, Pennsylvania. That camp at Rosedale was the first concession ever made by the United States government to conscientious objectors and was the forerunner of the Civilian Public Service Camps administered during World War II by Friends, the Brethren, and the Mennonites.

In that period of absence from Glens Falls, Murray also helped with the organization of the American Friends Service Committee and served as its first Personnel Secretary. That service was a small but significant one and the first of his many pioneering efforts as a Friend.

At that time in his life, Murray Kenworthy was a sturdy, strong, solidly-built individual, weighing around 175 pounds. He was five feet, ten inches tall–a good height in those days–and he had sandy hair with a tinge of red, probably inherited from his mother, Hannah Stout Kenworthy. Most of his life he wore a moustache, but never a beard except for the few days already mentioned.

He was a friendly, outgoing person and often stopped to talk to people on the sidewalks. He was well-known for his stories and witty comments. Often there was a twinkle in his eyes which was one of his especially appreciated characteristics.

After three years in Glens Falls, Murray was invited to go to Wilmington, Ohio, to become the executive secretary of Wilmington Yearly Meeting.

That was a challenging assignment, and he readily accepted it. One reason for his acceptance was the fact that it would take him back to the Midwest near his parents in New London, and to Lenora's mother in Spiceland.

Having grown to a population of five thousand, Wilmington had just been declared a city by the state of Ohio. It was the county seat of Clinton County, a trading center for an agricultural area of southwestern Ohio, and the location of several factories and firms. Among them were the Swaim Canning Company which specialized in high-grade sweet corn, the Wilmington Casting Company which had been started by a former employee of the National Cash Register Company in nearby Dayton, the Fisher Manufacturing and Fuel Company which specialized in lumber and building supplies, the Irwin Auger Bit Company, the Farquhar Furnace Company, and the Clyde C. Beam Company which dealt with crushed stone.

The story of the settlement of southwestern Ohio by Friends is similar to the one already outlined about Friends in parts of Indiana. Opposed to slavery, Friends in North and South Carolina and Tennessee moved into the Northwest Territory soon after the Ordinance of 1787 was enacted, outlawing that evil institution in the territory. In places they were joined by Quakers from Pennsylvania. In southwest Ohio they found fertile farmland, some of the soil dropped by the giant glaciers which had once covered that area. The remnants of Indian settlements were also much in evidence, with 256 Indian mounds located in Clinton County.

Many of the Quaker settlers used the Ohio River as their highway. Then they followed the well-marked Indian trails (such as the Bullskin and the Pickawillany) on the edge of what eventually became Clinton County. Others followed the east-west trail which later became the roadway between Chillicothe, the first capital of Ohio, and western Indiana.

There were still many Indians in that region, but the early Quakers immediately made friends with them. There was never a single incident of trouble in Clinton County between the red men and the white men. Referring to that relationship, Howard Brinton wrote in *Children of Light* that "The Indians so appreciated this friendly and just service that they coined the expression, the Quakers and the other white people."

Several Quaker communities were formed early in the history of southern Ohio. The most important was certainly Miami Monthly

Meeting in what is now Waynesville, set up in 1803 as the first monthly meeting of Friends in the Northwest Territory. According to the records of that monthly meeting, 220 monthly meetings, indulged meetings, and preparative meetings were formed by it. That is an astonishing number and a little known fact in the history of American Quakerism.

Another important Quaker center was Fairfield, a country meeting near Leesburg. One newspaper account of a summer session of Fairfield Quarterly Meeting in the early 1800s stated that it drew ten thousand people. Of course most of them did not come to attend the meetings for worship or to take part in the business sessions. They came to enjoy themselves; it was a good excuse for people to get together. Fairfield became known in more recent times by the prominence in Wilmington Yearly Meeting and in the Five Years Meeting of various members of the Terrell family. Among the other early Friends meetings in that part of Ohio were Center, Chester (probably named for a Meeting in Pennsylvania), Dover, Caesar's Creek, Fall Creek, Springfield, and Grassy Run.

From a historic point of view the most interesting Friends community was New Vienna, as it had once been the location of the first Quaker publishing house in the United States. In it *The Christian Worker* (a forerunner of *The American Friend*), *The Messenger of Peace,* Sunday School aids, and many tracts had been produced around the turn of the century.

When Murray moved his family to Wilmington, Ohio, the yearly meeting there was one of the most compact Quaker groups in the United States, a little like the large number of meetings around Philadelphia. There were forty-four local monthly meetings in the yearly meeting, of which about half were in Clinton County. All but six were within a radius of fifty miles of Wilmington. Those thirty-eight monthly meetings were parts of three quarterly meetings-Center (Wilmington), Fairfield, and Miami.

The other six monthly meetings were in Friendsville Quarterly Meeting in Tennessee. They were the remnants of a large Quaker group which had lived in that region prior to the mass migration into the Northwest Territory, plus one monthly meeting (Oak Grove) in the Great Smoky Mountain area, plus a few "chapels" or outposts nearby.

In addition to its two elementary schools and high school, it was the location of Wilmington College. The Campbellites had started an institution of higher learning in Wilmington in the 1860s, called Franklin College. They had not been able to make a go of it financially, and it came under the auspices of Friends in 1870.

Wilmington Yearly Meeting had been set off from Indiana Yearly Meeting in 1892, largely as a result of the acquisition of Wilmington College. Its total membership in the early 1920s was 6,400. Of that number 1,100 were members of the Wilmington Friends Meeting, the second largest Quaker group in the United States. Its minister or pastor was Earle J. Harold, a graduate of Earlham College in the class of 1899. His wife, Clara O'Neil Harold, was a graduate of the class of 1900 in which Murray and Lenora Holloway Kenworthy were members.

The first two homes of the Kenworthys were on the edge of the college campus. Across the street was the auditorium and sports arena of the college and the site of the yearly meeting sessions. Nearby were the football and baseball fields which we Kenworthy boys enjoyed tremendously.

Carroll was still in Oakwood School but entered Earlham College in the fall of 1921, to the dismay of some Wilmington Yearly Meeting Friends who thought that the son of their executive secretary should have enrolled in the local college. But Earlham was the Kenworthy and Holloway family institution, and it was Carroll's choice to go there.

Wilmer and I walked to school on the other side of town, a considerable distance. Then one evening the superintendent of schools had dinner in our home and in the course of conversation inquired where we attended school. When he was told, he commented that our second home was in a different district from our first one and that we should be attending another school. So we transferred, much to our annoyance. What a difference one dinner can make in one's life! Later, however, the Kenworthys purchased a house on Mulberry Street, near the center of town, and we returned to our first school. Whether that purchase was made at least in part because of the school situation, none of us knows.

Anyway, we inherited in that place a large rabbit hutch which provided us with rabbits for our meals and some to sell. In addition, Wilmer and I had our own plots of ground on which we raised radishes and onions and sold them door-to-door in carefully prepared bunches. We also sold tickets to the winter and summer Chautauquas, a form of recreation and education still popular in those days. We received free tickets when we reached the established quota.

Although Wilmington Yearly Meeting was, for the most part, compact geographically, it was not so religiously. Most of the meetings had pastors, and their services were very much like those in other Christian denominations, with the exception of the short periods of silence observed in some of them. But there was at least one meeting which still held its meetings for worship on the basis of silence, although there was some singing. And there were at least two that were highly evangelical. I recall attending one of them when the older people prayed on their knees in the front of the room while the young people sat on the back row and snickered. It was my first–and only–experience of such a highly evangelical Quaker group.

Since nearly all of those meetings had pastors and many of them could not afford a full-time worker, one of Murray's main tasks was to locate people who felt that they could give at least part-time to such work, whether they were teachers, farmers, storekeepers, or bankers. Meetings often needed to find new pastors, too, to replace those who had moved within the yearly meeting or to another yearly meeting. That work took considerable time and effort–and sometimes some diplomatic negotiations. In that connection, he was always on the lookout for promising young people who could be encouraged to be ministers. Sometimes he succeeded; Ralph Boring, a young man from Tennessee was one of those young men who entered the ministry, partly as a result of being found by Murray.

Murray Kenworthy believed in the pastoral system for many meetings. He believed, too, that it was likely to continue in Wilmington Yearly Meeting and in other parts of the United States. As he had already been a pastor, he knew its potentialities–and its problems. Therefore he felt it could be vastly improved, especially by the education of ministers or pastors. Therefore he developed what might be called a five-pronged program for pastors.

First, he believed in the importance of a rigorous study of the Bible, of Christianity and of Quakerism, and of contemporary social issues.

Second, he was concerned that Friends not continue to mimic other denominations, doubting if Quakers could compete or should compete with other groups in most aspects of programmed worship. He therefore urged the ministers of the yearly meeting to think about and experiment with types of worship which would be more spontaneous than ones they had previously used–with longer periods of silence or "open worship" and the encouragement of so-called laymen to take part vocally in those quiet times. Today the popular term for such an approach is "the enabling ministry."

Third, he thought that since there were going to be sermons, they should be well-prepared and should speak to the condition of all the members and attenders of the meeting. This was a field in which he was already an acknowledged expert, and he tried to share his approach and his training with others, individually and in small groups. He believed firmly and said often publically that God could and did speak during the week. His messages were not confined to periods of quiet worship on Sundays.

Coupled with this was his concern about the pastoral work of ministers, and he developed what would be called today "the case-study" method, using situations with which he was familiar outside the local area, lest persons and problems be easily identified.

Fourth, he felt deeply that Friends should not be trapped by the contemporary tendency to reject the findings of science and religious scholarship about evolution and higher criticism. Quietly and judiciously, yet persistently, he sought opportunities to present those views.

Finally, he wanted all of those approaches to be undergirded and buttressed by a good liberal arts education. In that respect he urged individuals to take courses in Wilmington College, or in other institutions. Often Murray loaned his own books or arranged for books to be loaned by libraries to the ministers in the yearly meeting. Complementing all he did with individuals and with groups was the teaching he carried on part-time in the Biblical Department of Wilmington College where he conducted courses in religious education and in the Christian ministry.

There is no record of how many meetings he visited, but he was certainly faithful in that regard. Often he attended one meeting in the morning and another in the evening, sometimes visiting people or sitting with committees in the afternoon. And what has been said about postal carriers applied equally to him—that neither snow nor rain nor darkest night could keep him from his appointed rounds.

On many occasions he took Wilmer or me with him, partly to have some company and partly to have more time with us as a father. Even though I was only 7, 8, or 9, I recall something today about most of the meetings in that yearly meeting.

Then, on Sunday evenings we would often have a light supper and a time together. Occasionally Dad would blindfold Wilmer and me and give us newspaper "bats" made by rolling the sheets together. We would grab each other's hands in order to know where we were approximately—and then try to swat each other. Or he would take on both of us in this simple home-made game, calculated in part to take some of the excess energy out of his growing boys!

At other times we would gather around the piano while Mamma played such favorite hymns as "Day is Dying in the West" or "Jesus, Savior, Pilot Me."

Another aspect of his job as executive secretary of the yearly meeting was to help educate Friends about the work of Quakers in the wider world as they tried to carry out their concerns on peace, prisons, education, and other topics. I recall, for example, one bitter cold night when Dad, Mamma, and I drove in our Model T Ford to the Springfield Meeitng out in the country. Only a few Friends were present, but Dad went anyway because he had promised to show stereoptican slides of the mission work of the Five Years Meeting. We drove back over icy roads with the wind howling. When we arrived on Mulberry Street, we were all exhausted. Dad then carried me into the house even though I was "a big boy" by then. It is an experience I have never forgotten.

To make such trips more tolerable, he devised special oilcloth curtains which could be fastened onto the car, with tiny isinglass windows. And for our family trips he cut loose and then hinged the back of the front seat so that it could be let down and made into a bed at night. Then he devised wooden boxes which could be fit onto the running boards and into which our camping equipment could be stored.

An important part of his work was the oversight of the meetings in Friendsville Quarterly Meeting in Tennessee. Since 1897 those meetings had been a part of Wilmington Yearly Meeting, transferred at their request from North Carolina Yearly Meeting. Two of those meetings were Lost Creek and Hickory Creek–groups which remained after the mass exodus to the Northwest Territory (Lost Creek had been established in 1785). Then there was a meeting in Knoxville and the remnants of a once large meeting in Maryville where an enterprising evangelist had built up that group but where the meeting was now dying.

Friendsville was unique as it had been settled as a Quaker town in 1815 and boasted a school, Friendsville Academy, with around 150 students. Founded in 1857, it lasted until 1975–a very late date for such a school.

Oak Grove was the only established monthly meeting in the mountains of Monroe County. But there were four or five "chapels," which were under the care of Wilmington Yearly Meeting, with some help from the Home Mission Board of the Five Years Meeting.

From time to time Murray visited all those meetings. Then one summer, he, Mamma, and I spent a month or so in that area. That was my first exposure to "an economically underdeveloped region," and it made a lasting impression on me. The land was poor and the people were poor. Sometimes the farmers had to dig footholds on the sides of the hills in order to plant their crops and to weed them. Some farmers raised chickens and made butter, but they seldom ate those products; instead, they sold them as almost the only cash crops they had.

During our visit in Monroe County, we stayed in the home of the Best family, leading local Friends who owned the only house made of planed boards in the entire area. Even today I have vivid recollections of many new experiences in that region, such as the four-year-old grandson of a Baptist minister lighting his grandfather's pipe and taking a few puffs on it in the process. Or of the women sitting on their front porches, talking and chewing tobacco, spitting the tobacco juice through their fingers and out onto the lawn.

At another time I helped with the making of butter in an old-fashioned wooden churn. Placed in the nearby stream to cool, the swollen water took it downstream and the men had to walk quite a distance to find and retrieve it.

Several nights we went to nearby chapels for "special services" with Murray Kenworthy of Ohio preaching. At one of those meetings Dad prayed on his knees, and I was surprised, even shocked. When I asked him why he did that, he said that they would not have thought he was praying if he had not done so. Apparently he had learned to do in Rome (or Monroe County) what the Romans (or Monrovians) did. Traveling in various economically underdeveloped countries in many parts of the world later in my life, I have thought of such incidents–and hopefully profited by them.

As a person who had lived as a boy in near-frontier conditions, Murray was most sympathetic with the plight of those farmers and their families and anxious to do almost anything he could to improve their lot. The answer that he came up with was to find a dedicated Quaker farming couple who would help to develop a demonstration farm and serve the Oak Grove Meeting and the nearby chapels. It was a brilliant idea, a little like the Point Four or AID (Agricultural and Industrial Development) plans of the American government many years later.

Murray found just the right couple in J. Edward and Daisy Ransome, New York Yearly Meeting Friends he had known. He persuaded them to move to Monroe County, Tennessee, and to build a simple but "model" home, and to start a "demonstration farm," without calling it that. The Ransomes lived there for many years, serving the community in a variety of ways. Later vast changes took place in that area, especially when much of it became a part of the Shenandoah National Park.

One other experience needs to be told to indicate some of the changes occurring in midwest Quakerism at that time. Moving further and further away from many of the testimonies and practices of Friends, some Wilmington Yearly Meeting Quakers felt it would be more appropriate to call that group The Friends Church rather than the Religious Society of Friends. The suggestion came before the yearly meeting and was championed by J. Edwin Jay, the president of Wilmington College. Murray Kenworthy opposed it as a further modification of the unique mission of Friends. But he lost, and Wilmington Yearly Meeting added the phrase "of the Friends Church" to its title. It was a small change but indicative of other deeper shifts in emphasis at that time and in that place. Years later the original name was restored.

Murray Kenworthy had scarcely begun to dig his roots into the Quaker soil of southwestern Ohio when he was asked to serve with the American Friends Service Committee in the feeding program they and English Friends were undertaking in the Soviet Union. The man who asked him to go on that mission was Wilbur K. Thomas, an Indiana Friend who had graduated from the Friends University in Wichita, Kansas, and was then the executive secretary of the American Friends Service Committee. Wilbur Thomas knew Murray Kenworthy well and felt that no one was better qualified than he was.

It was a difficult decision in some ways for Dad and Mamma to make. It would mean leaving her with us in the United States while he went abroad to a land plagued with famine, disease, and political turmoil. It would mean leaving their three parents, at an advanced age, depriving them of Murray's support and counsel. It would mean leaving a job which had barely begun and to which he had given the last full measure of his skill and devotion.

Yet, in another way it was not a difficult decision to make. They felt that if young men could risk their lives in wartime, pacifists should be ready to risk their lives in peacetime. Writing later about the sacrifices soldiers make, Murray went on to say:

> Here was a challenge to do the same for the cause which Quakers were sponsoring and which would help this cause before the Christian and non-christian world, at the same time helping needy people. It seemed like the height of hypocrisy to preach one thing–urging others to the responsibility of venturing–and then, when one was challenged, to refuse a similar sacrifice.

He also commented that "It would be useless to express the emotional experiences in that decision." But their answer was affirmative; he would go.

Little did Dad and Mamma realize what that decision would involve. But sometimes it is important not to know what lies ahead.

RELIEF WORK IN THE SOVIET UNION

Late in September of 1921 Murray Kenworthy set off for the Soviet Union to take part in the famine relief work which English and American Quakers directed there. Frantically he and Lenora had completed their preparations for that trip and for his absence from his family. Carroll had been sent off to Earlham College where he would be a freshman. A.B. Cherry would take care of the small Kenworthy farm near Knightstown, Indiana. Grandma Holloway would spend the coming winter in Wilmington, and the work in the yearly meeting had been parceled out. Murray had taken the necessary "shots" and packed the little he could take with him for the next year.

He stopped in Philadelphia to consult with the staff of the American Friends Service Committee at its headquarters at 20 South 12th Street, and especially with its executive secretary, Wilbur K. Thomas. Then in New York City he had boarded the *Berengeria,* one of the largest vessels afloat at that time. The ship had been the German-owned *Imperator* until it had been seized by the British during World War I. The voyage across the Atlantic was "a great one." It must have been unusual as Murray was not accustomed to speaking or writing in superlatives.

Upon his arrival in Berlin, Murray consulted with the Quaker relief workers who had been feeding a million and a half children daily. Then he proceeded to Stettin and by boat to Riga, Latvia. For two days and three nights, their ship tossed and turned in turbulent waters. En route they passed two floating mines which were probably filled with enough explosives to sink a big battleship. They maneuvered past that "seablock," and thanked their stars that they had encountered it in the daytime rather than at night.

When in Latvia, Murray discovered that the visa which an office worker in Berlin had obtained for him was for Lithuania rather than for Latvia. Murray was taken to the police station. Fortunately the reputation of the Quaker work in Germany salvaged the situation, and he was allowed to proceed.

As Murray Kenworthy approached the Soviet Union, he must have thought about the many contacts Quakers had had with that country over a period of nearly three hundred years. The first major contact of Quakers with a future ruler of Russia was in 1697, when Peter the Great (1682-1725) traveled to London incognito as a part of his preparation for the westernization of his land. Friends contacted him in London and he attended a few Quaker Meetings there and in Germany. Later a member of a Quaker family of doctors, Thomas Dinsdale, was brought by Catherine the Great (1729-1796) to her domain and she was inoculated by him against smallpox in order to reassure her people that that was a satisfactory precaution against the dreaded disease.

In the early part of the nineteenth century William Allen, Stephen Grellet, Luke Howard, and others went to Russia to encourage Alexander I (1777-1825) in his peace efforts for Europe and to foster William Allen's interest in introducing the Lancastrian system of education which had been developed in Quaker schools in England. Also Daniel Wheeler, a British Friend, was in charge of the reclamation of the desolate marshes around St. Petersburg for fifteen years and taught agriculture in Russia at the invitation of Alexander I. In the middle of the nineteenth century John Bright and Joseph Sturge, two Quaker statesmen, had tried valiantly to prevent the Crimean War between England, France, Sardinia, and Russia in 1854–1856.

As recently as 1906, British Friends had supported some famine relief work in the vast Volga area, although they had not administered such aid. Then came World War I and the Russian Revolution of 1917, overthrowing the Czarist regime and replacing it with a communist government. During the war, thousands fled from Poland when Warsaw was taken over by the Germans. Added to that mass of humanity were the retreating Russian soldiers. It is estimated that three million men, women, and children fled from their homes, most of them heading eastward towards Moscow and other Russian cities. Adding to all that confusion, turmoil, and misery were the droughts in the Volga valley where millions of people starved.

British Friends were able to supply some knitted clothing, to start orphanages, and to establish small lending libraries. In addition, they tried to establish an industrial school for boys but their efforts were thwarted and terminated.

A small unit of American Friends did reach Russia in 1917 by way of Japan and Siberia, after being detained for weeks in Tokyo. But further work was disrupted by the local political situation and by the Allied blockade which lasted until the summer of 1921. The British were able to dispatch a small unit and start relief work there in 1920, but only Arthur Watts, a British Quaker, and Anna J. Haines, an American, were permitted to stay. That small unit was termed by Fritjof Nansen, the Norwegian explorer, statesman, and champion of refugees, "The Flying Column."

By the fall of 1921, there was a breakthrough, and several British Friends were able to resume relief work. Then a small group of American Quakers was allowed to go to the Soviet Union to work. It was as a part of that American contingent that Murray Kenworthy had made the trek from the U.S.A. to the Soviet Union in the fall of 1921.

As soon as he arrived in Moscow, Murray caught his first glimpse of the severity of conditions there and imagined how much worse they would be outside the capital. Writing home, he said:

> Moscow is the dirtiest, dreariest, and most dilapidated city I
> have ever seen. And it is COLD. Seven years of war,
> revolution, riots, famine have taken a fearful toll. It is full of
> people from the outside, thousands of whom have come here
> in the hope, somehow, of finding food.

In the railroad station he saw thousands of people entering the city, believing there would be more to eat in Moscow than elsewhere. And they were right. The government was determined to feed its workers and to create as good an impression on the foreigners there as they could. Nevertheless, conditions were miserable.

In many instances fathers and mothers had packed their children into special coaches provided by the government for children. In one such train Murray saw a special two-tiered platform which had been built in a freight car with children huddled like chickens in a coop on the way to market. Of course the parents realized that they might never see their offspring again, but they were willing to let them go, hoping that somehow their lives would be saved.

British and American Quakers decided to divide the work with the Americans working in the Minsk and the Samara districts. Cornell and Estelle Hewson went to Minsk to direct the work there and Murray Kenworthy proceded to the Samara area. At first it had been hoped that Clement Biddle, a well-known Philadelphia Quaker businessman, would be named chief of the mission. But he had decided not to go to the Soviet Union and Murray became acting chief, then chief of the American delegation, and finally chief of the British and American relief missions.

The American contingent was very small at first, but it grew rapidly and eventually became a sizeable group, including several well-known Quakers. Among them were Homer and Edna Morris (who served on the faculty of Earlham College for many years, then, with the AFSC), Harry and Rebecca Timbres (who later went to India and then in the 1930s back to the U.S.S.R. for an extended stay), Oscar Moon, Beulah Hurley, Miriam West, Nancy Babb and Perry Paul.

The Samara area was in the eastern part of European Russia and covered a region extending eight hundred miles north and south and four hundred miles east and west. That would make it the equivalent of Minnesota, Wisconsin, Iowa, and Illinois. In 1921, 70 percent of the land in that region had failed to produce anything, and the remaining 30 percent had produced only 1 1/4 bushels of wheat per acre. And that was in the heart of the Volga district of the U.S.S.R., "the bread basket" of Russia, comparable to the Mississippi Valley in the U.S.A. or the pampas in Argentina. Consequently, an estimated fifteen million people were starving, utterly dependent on outside help.

When Murray reached Buzuluk, he faced a situation which was beyond anything he had imagined. If the train station in Moscow was packed, it was even more crowded in Buzuluk. Even the empty or near-empty freight cars on the sidings were crowded with people hoping that those cars would eventually be moved. People even perched on the engines of the trains. Those people did not care where the trains were headed. "Anywhere" was better than "here." They were desperate to leave the horrible conditions where they lived and hoped somehow that life would be better "out there." If they did not succeed in crowding onto a moving vehicle, they often huddled under the loading platforms, sometimes making makeshift "houses" by placing pieces of cloth between them and their neighbors.

Sometimes pandemonium reigned when a new train chugged into the station. People would dash for it, determined somehow to get on board. Frequently there were soldiers on hand with fixed bayonets to control the mobs and prevent riots. As Murray wrote home, "It has to be seen and experienced to be believed. The only words I can use to describe such conditions are horrid or unbelievable."

According to his accounts, however, he had not fully realized what hunger and famine meant until he got out into the villages of the Samara district. In them, he noticed at once that the straw had been removed from the roofs of all or almost all the houses in order to feed the animals–and later, the people. Often it was combined with weeds or bark to make what they called "bread." In other places people used chopped lime leaves, birch leaves or dried grass, mixed with horses hoofs, for bread.

It must have been almost impossible for the staff workers to eat their meals when they realized what was going on around them. But they had to eat or they could not help. Therefore Murray began to pull the curtains of the room where they ate because people came to watch them. Meat was non-existent, except for the flesh of their dead animals.

That was not all that he learned. He discovered that some desperate people had turned to cannibalism. Of course he dared not say so in his letters lest they be read by the censors and their work be terminated or some of them sent back to the States. But he did suggest that Mamma and Grandma Holloway might read II Kings 6:25-31.

I don't think they read that passage aloud, but that section of Kings related a grim story of a pact between two women during a famine in Israel. By it they agreed to eat their sons. They ate one and then the other woman hid her son so that he would not suffer a similar fate. The application to the Soviet situation was very clear.

Of course death was at the doorstep of every house constantly. And when the winter came, with its sub-zero weather (sometimes as low as fifty degrees below zero), death walked into the homes of most families. Hundreds died. Thousands died. Here is an excerpt from another of his letters regarding the dead:

> When I arrived in the Samara region there were already dead bodies in the street. For a time they were gathered up every morning or so and their clothing stripped from their bodies. Then they were hauled to the cemetery where large, square holes had been dug. Into them the bodies were piled, first side-by-side and then the next group crosswise until the hole was nearly filled. Then a thin layer of earth was thrown over the top.

> Soon, however, there were not enough able-bodied men to

keep pace with the deaths, and the bodies were thrown out in piles, in much the same way that a farmer might throw out four-foot cordwood.

Then, when winter came, the dead bodies were not buried until our clean-up corps could do that in the spring.

Imagine what that meant, also, in the spread of diseases. Such searing details were kept from Wilmer and me, but little boys can have big ears, and we occasionally overheard remarks between Mamma and Grandmother Holloway which taught us more than we needed to know about such words as "famine," "hunger," "pestilence," and "disease."

What does one write home to two lads, ages 13 and 9, when one is carrying on relief work in a hunger-filled land? One cannot just write a series of questions about how is your school, the Sunday School, your games, and other forms of fun.

So Dad finally composed a letter to Wilmer and me describing a typical village—one named Andrefka. He omitted the lurid details about famine, toned down his verbs, and avoided any adjectives he might have been tempted to use. Instead, he said that Andrefka dated back hundreds of years. To illustrate that point he said that the road running through it had been worn so long that it was like half of a hollow log. In that hollow, the water often collected, including water from the nearby yards where the stock were kept. (It didn't take much imagination to figure out that he was talking about polluted water). The water was often so bad that he and his friends always boiled their water before they drank it or even used it to brush their teeth.

Then he told about the houses which were largely made of split logs, usually with straw roofs (no mention that the straw had been used to make bread). Occasionally, however, there were houses with metal roofs. Other houses were made of mud or sun-dried-brick-clay in which short lengths of straw had been mixed. Those houses were small and had low entrances in the rear. Floors were packed earth. In them, there was always a stove into which "bricks," made from dried manure and then dried in the sun, were thrown as fuel. That, he continued, made a hot fire but emitted a terrible stench which often hurt his throat.

In the center of the village was an open market where everything was sold, from neckties to a load of hay. That market was open every day, but when the temperature dropped many degrees below zero, people often stayed at home.

Near the market was the village church—called the Russian Orthodox—which he said was something like the Roman Catholic

Murray Kenworthy Writes Home

FRIENDS' INTERNATIONAL SERVICE
ОБЩЕСТВО ДРУЗЕЙ (КВАКЕРЫ). ОТДЕЛ ПОМОЩИ ДЕТЯМ.

СКЛАД № 5 ЦЕНТРОСОЮЗА.
ПЕРЕВЕДЕНОВКА.
ИНСТРУМЕНТАЛЬНЫЙ ПЕР. 7
МОСКВА = Moscow
Moskva

ТЕЛЕФОН №
ЧАСЫ ПРИЕМА: 2 Ч. Д.—4 Ч. Д.

Moscow
Russia

№

Dear Parents   11 / 5 192 1

We have been here in Moscow just over one week, getting in here
about three in the afternoon and now it is eight. We are soon to leave
for our respective fields of work. The Hewsons had expected to go to
Minsk last night but did not get government permission in time so will
probably get off next Tuesday night - two trains a week only. We have
$95000 worth of food stuffs there to be distributed and no Friend on
the job, there are two Russians looking after the stuff for the present.
This is to go to childrens homes and will last about three months. We
hope the ARA (Russian) JDC (Jews) will make a contribution to continue
this work for there are many Jews there, in fact some of these homes are
mostly filled with Jewish orphans. This food, that is there, was bought
with JDC money. (American) Jewish Distribution Committee.

I am to go on to Buzuluk to morrow afternoon, with three English
workers, one of them the Chief, also our American acting chief, named by
us, since we came here, and to act until our head man comes. His name is
Arthur Watts. One of these three is an American, a doctor, who has come in
here, thru Siberia, from China. She offered to work with Friends and the
English accepted her.

We American Friends had to come in as part of the ARA personnel
but were to be given a definite are in which to work; we have however
arranged to continue with the English Friends, and will continue to
work as the Anglo-American Friends work or as stated in the heading
above. We will keep separate books, and may have definite distributing
points but will not attempts to keep our rations. separate, nor be very
discriminating as to where our workers are stationed- that is we may
have English and Americans working at the same point.

I do not know much about conditions down at B- only that they
are desperate, Parents are dying in large numbers, leaving their children
a little food in the hope that some one will bring them more food so
they at least can live on, or they have taken them to the centers where
there are childrens homes and left them there in the hope that they can
get into the homes. Often houses intended to house 40 children have 4x
or 5 times that many. There is little or no food for them, no soup, no
medicine, and ten or a dozen children die in a day and are carted off
in rude carts to be buried or - . The adults have been making a kind of
bread out of powdered grass or any kind of vegetable with a little
grain flour in it, now the snow has gone and the little grass is to be

to be found is covered and thousands will lie where formerly there were
hundreds. Arthur Ransome, a noted newspaper correspondent, says in the
Manchester, England, Guardian that the people even make a tea out of
horse dung and drink it. I presume I will know more about the situation
from having seen it by this time next week. Of course I may not reach
Buzuluk by that time. I may be held up here for some cause as the H²
have been. Or as is sometimes the case the old engine may blow up or
break down on the way. But we expect to make the trip in about three
days or less, it is something over 1000 miles down there.

We are very pleasantly housed here in Moscow, we now have warm

Church in Wilmington. It was still being used in 1921, and he had attended services there. But he told us that it had no seats and that people stood during the three-hour service, although almost no one stayed for that entire time. Instead, they dropped in and out as they pleased. (We rather liked that idea and wished they would do that in Wilmington even for our one-hour service.)

Giving us a little history, he remarked that such villages had existed in the Soviet Union for hundreds of years. Originally they were to protect people against their enemies and to provide for sociability. Otherwise the farmers and their families might be lonely if they lived on separate farms. People lived in the village and went out to their work each day, in somewhat the same way that Grandpa Kenworthy drove his horse, "Charlie," out to the farm almost daily to work with the man who lived there.

He also pointed out that in "normal times" the children worked hard and had little time or energy to play. We noticed that he had nothing to say about schools, and Mamma explained that schools were rare there.

He could have added that the collectivization of the farms had not taken place, that the local church had not yet been closed, or other changes instituted yet. But that letter was written to young boys to let them know where their father was and that he was interested in them despite the vast distance that separated them. A treatise on the political situation was therefore out of place and could have been dangerous for him to write.

Despite the incredible conditions in the Soviet Union, much could be done, and much was done, to help. First, there were parents, relatives, neighbors, and friends working and—often giving up their lives so that children could be saved. The Communist government also helped. After all, they were interested in the health of their children and future citizens. What would the U.S.S.R. be without them? Therefore large sums of money were expended to fight the famine and bring relief to as many people as possible—children first. Orphanages and children's centers were enlarged and/or created, and it was in those institutions that much of the Quaker feeding took place. Also, passenger trains were sidetracked so that shipments of food and other supplies could get to the hungry and the needy as soon as possible. At the ports, ships with food and other supplies were given the right of way.

There were also hundreds, perhaps thousands, of nameless persons who did what they could do to help. Dad wrote:

> I was at Alexiefka when the first flour arrived. A one-horse
> wagon had made the trip of 40 miles to Buzuluk and the 40

miles back. When it drew up to our door, it had but two large cotton bags of flour. When I inquired why there was not a large load, I was told that the horse was too weak to pull more.

How many horses, oxen, and cows died in the service that winter–I wonder? How many drivers dared the sub-zero weather to the point of 55, and the deep snows and raging blizzards– only to be frozen–I do not know. It was an awful winter and many died in the attempts to help alleviate the suffering.

In such a situation there were agonizing decisions to be made. What should be done? Who should be helped? Should time be spent on feeding or the same amount of time devoted to writing back to Philadelphia the story of the need so that more money could be raised? On a personal level, a family letter hinted at the anguish:

A few minutes before I began to write, I was lying in my room when a half-starved lad of about 18 appeared at our door. Of course I had to send him away. What will become of him–God only knows.

They come every day and usually they don't get past the doorman. But sometimes they do.

Are we hard-hearted? I sometimes wonder.

Dad didn't mention what it would be like to be a doorman turning down hungry people all the time. It would drive most of us wild; perhaps it drove that man mad later.

The answers to most of these questions were clear; it was the children who were to receive help first. The Russian government said so. The relief organizations said so. And the contributors said so. In fact, that decision had been made in all the other countries where relief work had been administered or was being administered then. In the U.S.A., for example, most people would not give a nickel to feed Communist adults, but many would give for children.

It sounds reasonable at first to save the lives of children. But was it? A comment from Dad questions that policy. He wrote:

Growing children in Russia (and elsewhere) could not maintain growth and health on the food that could be provided; they were subject to rickets and other diseases. On the other hand, older people, with more experienced constitutions, possibly could have endured and lived on the food we could have given them.

Actually there are times when it is a waste of food to save certain children. In fact, there are even times that children are so far gone that any food we give them may kill them.

Further on that point he wrote:

Should we be limiting our work to those areas or villages where we can care for the entire population? Should we take care of only families where there are children so that we can save many children and only need to save two adults?

Or would it be better to concentrate on young people–perhaps those of the age bracket of 15-25–so that they can propogate the race?

At another time he wondered if by feeding only children they were raising a generation of orphans in that part of the world. Upon his return to the U.S.A., he would ask if they were merely saving children so that they could be raised as Communists. He even wondered if it would have been better to have saved adults who might have been more likely to oppose the Communist regime. Questions, questions, questions–with no easy answers and probably no answers at all.

Despite all these questions and doubts and misgivings–ones which would haunt him the rest of his life–there were two major decisions. One was to feed the children, and the other was to start feeding in the distant and isolated villages. People in the larger centers were more likely to find access to food brought in from other parts of the Soviet Union or from abroad.

And what did they feed them? Here is Dad's answer to that query:

We only supply one meal a day and that meal costs us about three cents for each recipient. (If they get anything more, their parents or the government supplies it).

The contents vary, depending upon the gifts received from abroad and whatever can be obtained locally or in the U.S.S.R. Usually there is some kind of bread, a soup made of rice or corn grits, milk and sugar. Now and then there is a little meat. Sometimes there is a drink of cocoa. In the region served by English Quakers they sometimes have herring which has been given by the Norwegians or Swedes–or a little piece of chocolate from England (probably from one of the Quaker chocolate companies–the Cadburys, the Frys, or the Rowntrees). And the children have to be induced to eat the chocolate as they have never eaten it.

Fats are difficult to get, although badly needed. People even follow the trains to pick up the drops of oil from the engines. Then, off and on, cod liver oil is available and is spread on bread–such as we use syrup at home.

You can imagine what happened in a village when the word got out that the American Quakers were going to start feeding their children. Immediately the number of boys and girls in the orphanages and special homes swelled five or six times. People even brought their children and left them outside those institutions, thinking that the caretakers would not turn them away if they thought they had been abandoned.

The only reference I find to the number of children fed was in a report for the spring of 1922 when a passing comment was made on the 160,000 boys and girls in the care of the AFSC workers. Letters home indicate that Murray thought that was too high a figure.

It was not just food that was needed. Almost everything was in short supply. New clothing was non-existent, as little had been produced inside the Soviet Union for a long time, and no shipments had been received from abroad for seven years. In desperation, people used the clothes of those who had died, turned old flour sacks into trousers or suits, or devised other means of clothing themselves. Often a family had but one pair of shoes.

Some relief came with a shipment of raw wool from Australia. It was spun into yarn. The women who did that work were given a small quantity for their services, plus a ration of food for their "wages."

Horses were desperately needed, too, and members of the Friends Unit went to Siberia and Turkestan to purchase them to till the soil. On that expedition, two Quaker men lived for weeks in the skin tents of the Kirghis nomads, eating meals of fat mutton and mares' milk. Fodder for the draft animals also had to be sought outside the famine area.

In the spring, fifteen tractors were purchased in Poland for the plowing. That was a small number in the face of the need, but it was all they could obtain. In that same season the government sent trainloads of seed corn into the Buzuluk area, sidetracking passenger trains and even trains carrying food because of the urgency of having a new crop.

Added to the other difficulties of life at that time in the Soviet Union was the fact that travel was incredibly involved and slow. No matter where the relief workers went and how far they were traveling, they took their supplies with them–food, candles for lighting their compartments, bedding, and a primus stove for cooking. At each station they would rush to the "kipytock station" for the tea that the Russians drank in great quantities. Because the water was unsafe, the relief workers always drank tea, coffee, or cocoa. Murray pointed out that he never drank a drop of unboiled water in all the months he was in the U.S.S.R.

In the trains the small compartments were often shared with other travelers. In one of his few negative comments in his letters home he said:

> Men and women occupy these rooms, whether friends or strangers. And the Bolsheviki are not sensitive in matters of sex. In fact they are as free as cattle.

He added that train trips almost always provided some adventure. The engines usually burned oil, but there were always wooden stoves in the coaches. When they were stoked, hundreds of tiny sparks would fly in the dark. On one such trip rotted wooden beams of one coach caught fire and it was not put out until a large section had burned. Sometimes the engines used wood, and when it had been taken from the snow and ice, one never knew if the engines would keep the trains moving.

Because of these and other difficulties, train travel was unbearably slow. The trip between Buzuluk and Moscow was about a thousand miles but ordinarily it took two-and-a-half days. The equipment was often old and frequently broke down. In one account Murray reported that it had taken him ten days to make that trip, forty-eight hours of it spent in a railroad roundhouse, getting repairs.

Nevertheless, he was full of praise for the railroad men. For example, he reported that:

> It was an awful winter and there were often heavy snows that sometimes stalled the trains which, if caught in cuts, engulfed the entire train. In a few instances that situation caused the death of the entire crew and passengers. In addition, the train men were hungry and often so weak that heavy work was difficult if not impossible. At one time it was reported that about a third of the entire eastern service crew was stricken with typhus.

Commenting further on how they helped with the supplies that were being shipped, he said:

> In spite of weeks of sub-zero weather, snow, blizzards, hunger, and typhus, they got our supplies through as fast as they arrived in Moscow. It often took days to get a freight train from Moscow to Buzuluk, using any old engine that they could find. In fact our first food train from Buzuluk to Sorochenskoe was pulled by a passenger train engine while the entire passenger train was left on a siding while our goods were being delivered.

Murray's brother, Earl, apparently wrote him, or asked him through other members of the family, to explain why there was a famine of such proportions in a region of the U.S.S.R. which was reputed to be one of the finest agricultural areas in the world.

Murray's reply was long. First of all, the rain does not always fall in the vast Volga region and that had happened for two consecutive seasons. Murray asked Earl to imagine what would happen in the United States if the crops failed throughout the entire area of Iowa, Kansas, and the two Dakotas.

Then he pointed out that the Soviet Union had only one major crop in that region (wheat), whereas the Americans have two (corn and wheat). Therefore, if one crop fails in our country, there is still some chance that the other will be bountiful or at least adequate. In the Soviet Union, if the crop failed, all was lost.

To those two explanations Murray added the fact that for seven years there had been war, revolution, and civil war—the latter fomented in part by the United States. The consequence was the fact that an estimated twelve million persons had died. Of that number a high percentage were farmers, as the U.S.S.R. was almost exclusively an agricultural country at that time.

Furthermore Murray pointed out that the Russian farmers used very primitive tools and farm methods, and had very small yields per acre. In addition, the government had sold some of the limited supply of grain in Europe in order to obtain foreign currencies with which to purchase other much-needed materials. The last item he mentioned was the fact that many of the kulaks or rich farmers had violently opposed the Communist regime. When they learned that it was going to take all of their surplus grain, they planted just enough for their own needs, with no surplus.

Then, in a statement which might have been dangerous had the censor read it carefully, Dad added:

I am not in sympathy with the ideals and methods of the present government, but it is nevertheless the best one that Russia has ever had.

He was critical of the Russian Orthodox Church, however, pointing out that, with few exceptions, it had failed to use its vast wealth to alleviate the dreadful conditions that existed. It claimed that the gifts to it had been gifts to God which could not be touched. Dad had a very different view of God than that.

Added to the psychological strains already mentioned, there was the ever-present danger of disease. Typhus–a disease contracted by the bite of body lice–was the greatest fear of all workers. The workers all wore silk underwear as one precaution, but many of them were stricken, nevertheless. In the Red Cross unit in Minsk, for example, thirteen of the twenty-five workers succumbed to that dread disease and one of them died. In the Quaker unit Arthur Watts, Oscar Moon, Beulah Hurley and others came down with typhus.

And Dad did, too. On December 30, 1921, Mamma received a cable through the office of the American Friends Service Committee in Philadelphia which she assumed was a belated Christmas greeting. Instead it read:

Cable received Quote Kenworthy ill typhus slight have sent nurse for Kenworthy Unquote they will do best possible for him will keep you informed other news Wilbur Thomas

Mamma, Grandma Holloway, and the two older boys may have understood the seriousness of that situation; I didn't. Typhus was The Grim Reaper and few foreigners over forty survived. At that time Murray was 48.

For twenty-five days he was in bed, much of that time delirious. An Austrian doctor and an English nurse were brought to Buzuluk, and he was given every conceivable care by Beulah Hurley and Miriam West, two American workers in that region. But his battle with death was serious and prolonged. He did recover, however, and although able eventually to resume his work, he was weak and weary for months.

In May of 1922, Mamma and Dad were already beginning to refer frequently in their letters to his return to the States in July, after the completion of the year he had promised to serve with the AFSC in the Soviet Union. His letters indicated how glad he was to be involved in the work there but how eager he was to return.

It had been a difficult year for Mamma. Carroll had kept the family car in Richmond so that he could occasionally spend a weekend at home to help in any way he could. Grandma Holloway was good company, but she was getting old and could not help a great deal.

Meanwhile the water in our well had been declared contaminated, and the city had run a sewer pipe through our front yard. In addition to that and other local problems, the man on our small farm in Indiana had caused considerable trouble, probably taking advantage of Dad's absence. Furthermore, the Kenworthys were living on a Service Committee subsistence allowance; I recall vividly how many meals we ate of hominy in order to keep our food costs down.

In May Mamma became ill. Her condition became serious, and Carroll hurried home. Meanwhile Earl and Clara Harold, Elsie and Ethel McCoy, and other friends and neighbors did all they could to help. However, on May 23, 1922, Mamma died. After a brief service in Wilmington, the family went to New London where there was another service before her burial in the Friends cemetery there. It was significant to some of us that she was buried while it was raining slightly, as she had always loved the rain.

Days later Dad received word of Mamma's death. What a blow that must have been, separated by thousands of miles and still recovering from his bout with typhus. He was released from his work in the U.S.S.R. and brought it to an end as best he could. Then he began his long, weary, lonesome journey back to the United States. That trip took weeks. Instead of the glad homecoming we had all looked forward to, there was a sad reunion. Dad returned haggard and thin, with his clothes hanging from his body. The first night after his return to New London, we all gathered in the living room for the regular family devotions. Then Dad broke down and sobbed. It was the only time in his life that I ever saw him cry.

The day after Wilbur K. Thomas had seen Dad off on the boat to Europe in September, 1921, he had written Mamma a letter in which he said in part:

> Murray has gone to help with one of the largest pieces of work that Friends have ever undertaken and the largest piece of religious service that any religious denomination has ever done. It is an opportunity that comes not once in a generation, but once in five or six generations. I am very glad that we live in a day when we can serve and really make an impression on the world. I trust that in all of the days to come that the peace of God which passeth all human understanding will be your portion all the time.

The Kenworthy Family in Glen Falls, New York, 1917
From Left: Lenora, Leonard, Carroll, Wilmer and Murray

The 1889 Earlham College Football Team
    Back row from left: Earl Barnes, manager; Murray Kenworthy, Ben Grave,
L.C. Peacock, captain; Albert Chapman, David Sutton, Warren Grifflin. Center
row: Clarence Clark, Albert Hastings, Bernard Henley, T.M. Elliott, Harvey
Schilling. Front row: Floyd Reeve, Emory Ratcliff, O.J. Binford, Pleasant
Unthank. (Courtesy Earlham College Archives.)

New London Meetinghouses
Russiaville, Indiana

The first meetinghouse was a log structure. It served as meetinghouse and school until it burned sometime before 1850.

The second meetinghouse was completed in 1853. The frame structure could seat almost one thousand people in its two rooms formed by a shuttered partition. It was torn down in 1903 to make room for a more modern building.

This new meetinghouse was completed in 1905 and served until 1951 when it was destroyed by fire.

The current meetinghouse is a stone structure. The first services were held in this meetinghouse on November 16, 1952.

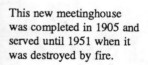

LECTURES

—ON—

INTERNATIONAL QUESTIONS

World War Debts
International Courts of Justice
American Exclusion and the Orient
The American Policy of Isolation
Uncle Sam and the Caribbean Republics
The Future of Russia
Storm Centers

BY

Murray S. Kenworthy

Regional Secretary
American Friends Service Committee

MURRAY S. KENWORTHY IS A MINISTER IN THE RELIGIOUS SOCIETY OF FRIENDS (QUAKERS). IN 1921-22 HE SERV-
ED AS CHIEF OF THE CHILD FEEDING MISSION WHICH THE AMERICAN FRIENDS SERVICE COMMITTEE SENT TO
RUSSIA. IN THE ACCOMPANYING PICTURE HE IS SEEN DRESSED IN A RUSSIAN LEATHER SUIT, A GARB MUCH
USED, AT THAT TIME, BY BUSINESS MEN AND GOVERNMENT OFFICIALS. HE WAS PASTOR OF THE FRIENDS
CHURCH IN WASHINGTON, D. C., FROM 1923-28. AT THE PRESENT TIME HE IS THE REGIONAL SECRETARY FOR THE
AMERICAN FRIENDS SERVICE COMMITTEE IN THE EASTERN CENTRAL STATES, WITH HEADQUARTERS AT 304
COLLEGE AVENUE, RICHMOND, INDIANA.

AFSC Fundraising Poster

Murray S. and Violet Cosand Kenworthy

Three Generations of Kenworthys
    Milton, Leonard, and Murray attended the 1937 World Conference of Friends at Swarthmore College.

Upon her death he might well have written a similar tribute, telling about the christening by Fridtjof Nansen of the ship which was to carry him and his expedition to the Arctic. That dedication by Nansen was "To her who had the courage to christen this ship–and to remain behind."

FUNDRAISING FOR THE AFSC

Of course, there were difficult decisions because of Mamma's death. During that summer Carroll would attend the YMCA conference at Lake Geneva and work at Earlham College. Wilmer would stay with our Kenworthy grandparents and work some with Uncle Earl on his farm. I would stay with Grandpa and Grandma Kenworthy. I played in the sandbox Grandpa made for me and spent hours playing the piano as I tried to work through the traumatic experience of losing my mother. But what of the future? Obviously Carroll would continue in Earlham College. But what should be done with Wilmer and me?

The Service Committee asked Dad to spend the next few months touring the United States telling the story of the famine in the Soviet Union and the relief work being carried on there by British and American Friends. He had plenty of experience as a speaker; none as a fund-raiser. The feeling was that his story would be so compelling that the funds would be forthcoming once he told it. And they were.

With that prospect in view, Dad decided to enroll Wilmer and me in Westtown School (the boarding school of Philadelphia Yearly Meeting, Orthodox), twenty-five miles west of Philadelphia. With generous scholarship aid that would be possible, Dad decided to live near the

Westtown railroad station, a couple of miles from the school. In that way he could commute to the Philadelphia office of the AFSC, live with Friends, and see us from time to time, despite his travels.

He first found a room in the home of the parents of James Walker, a teacher at Westtown and later its principal for many years. A few months after that he moved nearer the railroad station to the home of William and Frances Harvey. At that time William Havey was the executive secretary of Philadelphia Yearly Meeting (Orthodox), so he and Dad had many common interests.

Even though Dad was on the road much of the time, he was able to visit us occasionally. Usually it was on Saturday afternoons. With him he almost always brought a box of chocolates from the Snellenberg store in Philadelphia, which we boys shared. That was one of Dad's few indulgences or "sins"–his sweet tooth.

At holiday time Wilmer and I sometimes stayed with "Uncle Elbert" and "Aunt Lieutta" Russell at Woolman House in Swarthmore, or with the Houghton family at Westtown. The Russells were good friends, former neighbors in Richmond, and adopted relatives. George Houghton was a close friend of Dad's from Cambridge days, and they had hiked together in the Green Mountains.

Meanwhile Dad toured the United States in much the same fashion that Chautaqua speakers and singers or vaudeville troupes combed the country. It was a strenuous assignment for anyone, let alone a man who had come close to death from typhus a few months before.

Perhaps the best way to report on Dad's speaking tour of the United States is to quote from an article in *The New Republic* for March 14, 1923. On its editorial page it printed the following article or commentary:

A Quaker in Main Street

A certain eminent man went to Russia last year at the height of the famine to investigate and report on conditions there. He went through the country in a Government Special with every comfort and luxury the Soviets could afford. It was cold in Russia and he did not leave that comfortable car; he made his observations from the window.

In the famine districts Quaker relief workers came to the train and begged him to go with them through the desolate and starving villages. He did not care to go. After all, there was the danger of typhus and of cholera. He could see quite enough from the car windows. He came home to America and gave a cheerful report.

We in America have seen the Russian famine from a very comfortable and much more remote car window. We have seen it from the train deluxe of our national comfort and prosperity. Shall we get out and risk a personally conducted tour with one of these Quakers? We risk only our mental comfort, after all; there is no danger of typhus at this distance.

Murray S. Kenworthy, until last summer Chief of the Russian Unit of the American Friends Service Committee, is going about the country with the story of what he saw in Russia. He works hard, hurrying from city to city, speaking as many times a day as he can get a hearing. He may well hurry for it is time and death he is racing with. He knows that in his province at least the famine is not broken, that conditions are little better than they were last year. And the Quakers have not enough money to keep even the people they are feeding alive now till harvest. Suppose we listen to him as he spoke the other day at a prominent women's club on one of our Main Streets.

It is the weekly luncheon and some of the members are a little vague about what they have come to heard. "The Russian Famine," one of the ladies flutters, "Isn't that rather gruesome? I thought it was Russian Folk Songs this week. And I made such an effort to come. I must have got it mixed up with the Persian Folk Songs in the lecture the other day. Charming, wasn't it? So unusual! Well, well, I suppose there is still a famine over there, but isn't it mostly over? But perhaps we ought to hear about it."

Kenworthy begins conventionally enough. His first few sentences might have been spoken by anyone. Perhaps you are a bit disappointed. He is in no way picturesque. He is a tall, weatherbeaten man, very direct and simple, with none of the arts and graces to help him tell his story; only his stark sincerity, the nakedness of his terrible knowledge.

And then, subtly, you realize that the atmosphere has changed;

it has become electric, tense, charged with an unknown voltage. He is speaking about Russia. He is saying what he came to say. Like a knife-edge that message rips through the husks of common matters, the trappings of common speech, cuts that smug atmosphere to the quick of your very soul. It is not a man speaking at all. Something elemental, appalling, speaks through him; it is the cry of Russia's agony. He speaks quietly of unspeakable things. He does not comment or color or sentimentalize. He lets the facts speak.

You think, perhaps, you knew something about Russia; you have read things about the famine. Never anything like this. It is a transfer of experience. "I suppose you never heard the cry of a starving child," says the Quaker. You have heard it after Kenworthy speaks; God forgive you if you ever forget it. The man has stepped aside, self-forgetful, forgotten. He bids you look for yourself into the famine districts, into that ghastly inferno of suffering and desolation and heroic fortitude. No art can paint that picture like the naked immediacy of his speech. And you look on in a kind of numbed horror, seeing what he has seen. What is it you see through those haunted eyes of his?

Samara, where whole villages died. A country of barren steppes, timberless, snowbound. A temperature 40 to 55 degrees below zero. No food but grass bread; no fuel but stable dung. Whole villages starving; the dead lying in the streets where they fell, or heaped like "cord-wood" in the churchyard—stripped of their last rags "for the dead do not need that which the living must have." Parents tie their famished children when they leave them at home alone, lest they do injury to each other. For in that country cannibalism is no strange thing; children have been known to set upon their playmates; even today there are people driven by hunger who keep alive on human flesh.

In the orphan homes there is no bedding or blankets; the children, dressed most of them only in little shirts, huddle together for warmth on the bare slats or boards. In some they live on the floor, so thick that a visitor entering must step over the little bodies. Homes crowded to suffocation, crowded so that starving and freezing babies must be turned away.

Those who bring them unload the sledges, leave the children in the snow before the doors and drive off. There is no chance of life for them at home; here someone may still have pity....In the courtyards are piled the dead children. Sledges drive around, collecting them in the mornings, but often the sledges are overladen, and they may be left lying there for days or weeks. There are no living children under three years.

Whom to save and whom to leave to die? With rations for only a fraction of the starving people, that is the terrible decision that the relief missions must face. "What would *you* do?"–he puts the problem to us. "Shall we save the strongest, the young people most capable of carrying on the race, of ploughing and sowing, letting the old people and the children die? Shall we save the children only–thus multiplying the already huge problem of an orphan population? If we save the children alone, who is to care for them? Single families? Selected villages?" At last the children are chosen, since without American food they are sure to die. Old people are tougher; they must take their chance.

And then the other side, the nameless heroisms! Those peasant fathers and mothers died before relief could reach them, leaving enough food in the house so that the children might hold on until the Quakers came. Those starving sledge-drivers, scarcely able to stand, who brought the children's food safe to its destination. Those bandits who would not touch the Quaker stores, desperate men as they were, when they understood that America had sent them to the starving Russian children. "Can we ask more of Russia?" Of the steadfast heroism of the relief workers we hear nothing. Only from a casual parenthesis, "That day I caught the typhus," do we gather how lightly men and women hold their lives to whom typhus is, as it was to this man, all in the day's work.

"There are whole regions," he ends, "where no relief has ever penetrated. In one village we know of, the people last fall, feeling they could not live till spring, went out to the churchyard and dug their own graves, knowing that no friends of theirs would be strong enough when the time came to dig them. We have had orders to extend our feeding to that district–but there is not enough food or money to carry these people through till the harvest."

Abruptly, without any appeal for money, he sits down. It is over. There is a dead silence; then a woman bursts out, "Tell us the quickest way to help." She is the lady of the folk songs, but she does not seem to want them any longer. There are a few other questions, a few announcements. The spell is broken and we find that we can laugh and chat about other things as we go on about our business and desire–such as it is.

But we have been strangely moved and when we go home we shall probably send a check to the Quakers–oh, small enough to be quite sure it does not interfere with any plans for our own amusement. Perhaps, after all, we might not be so careful this time; perhaps it wouldn't hurt us to cut out a few things. After all, those people are dying...and in torment...How shall we write that check?

How can a man endure it? This precipice of indifference, preoccupation, apathy? This beating against closed doors, closed souls? Appealing for a situation unthinkable from a plane of experience alien as another planet? And all the time, days passing, death gaining in the race. So the prophets of old must have spoken what the Lord put in their mouths. *Is it nothing to ye, O ye that pass by?*

Yet he is not embittered. Out of that frozen hell he has brought, incredibly, sanity and sweetness. What gives him this immortal patience?

"The sun set, but set not his hope"–Is it perhaps the grace of God?

–D.H.

Many were moved by Dad's message, as was this reporter or editorial writer for *The New Republic*. But some were not moved. They denounced any effort to save the Bolsheviks or Communists, even if they were children. "Let them die," they said.

Some wondered why Dad didn't get back to preaching, proclaiming the gospel, saving souls. To them Murray replied with deep conviction and utter sincerity that he felt he was about the Master's business, reminding them of His words as recorded in Matthew:

> ...for I was hungry and ye gave me to eat; I was thirsty and ye
> gave me drink,...naked and ye clothed me...Verily I say unto
> you, Inasmuch as ye did it unto one of these my brethren, even
> these least, ye did it unto me.

Others wanted to verify their interest and understandably posed
questions. For example, they wanted to know what guarantee there was
that the food actually reached the needy. To that Dad always replied that
there was some loss, some stealing, some pilfering. "Can you imagine
the temptation to take food when you and your loved ones are starving?" he would ask. But he quickly added that he had been amazed at
how little loss there was. Food and other supplies were carefully
guarded and, also, people were heroic in passing up food so that their
children could obtain it and live.

People asked, too, about the cooperation of the Communist
government. To that he replied that it was in their interest to promote
the feeding, on political if not on humanitarian grounds. He pointed out
that everything the Communists could do to help was to their
advantage; otherwise there would be revolts against their regime. They
weren't about to invite insurrections.

For three months Dad's fund-raising activities were interrupted so that
he could serve as acting secretary of the American Friends Service
Committee in the absence of Wilbur K. Thomas. With that exception,
he spent a year barnstorming, raising thousands of dollars and thereby
saving the lives of thousands of human beings. But that year was
enough, and he moved to a very different type of work when he moved
to Washington D.C. to work with the Friends in the nation's capital.

LIFE
IN THE
NATION'S
CAPITAL

In 1923 Murray Kenworthy accepted the invitation of the Irving Street Friends Meeting in Washington D.C. to serve as its pastor, or what today would be called its pastoral secretary. It was a difficult assignment, but, in retrospect, one of the most rewarding of the many experiences of his long and useful life. For a variety of reasons, chiefly because of work with the federal government, a good many Quakers had moved to Washington. At that time there were two Friends meetings in the nation's capital. One was the Hicksite meeting on Eye Street in downtown Washington; the other the Orthodox meeting on Irving Street in the Columbia Heights section.

The Eye Street group was slightly larger and its members more unified in their views and ways of worship. It was an unprogrammed meeting, held on the basis of expectant silence. Next door to it was a school which had originally been owned and administered by the meeting but which had been bought by Thomas Sidwell and was called the Sidwell Friends School.

The Irving Street Meeting was much more diverse, drawing its members and attenders from the wide variety of Orthodox Friends in the United States. There were several families from the Wilburite or

Conservative group, such as the Stantons, the Rouses, and the Wetherills. There were a few from what is now the Evangelical Friends Alliance, chiefly the Halls from Ohio Yearly Meeting (Damascus). And there were more from the pastoral groups of the Five Years Meeting (now the Friends United Meeting), such as the Browns, Hiatts, and Woodwards.

They worshipped, also, on the basis of silence, and that was most appealing to the Conservative Friends. But the ministry, while sometimes acceptable, did not meet the needs of all friends and tended to be monopolized by one or two recorded ministers. Those who found music a satisfying aspect of worship also were dissatisfied if not sometimes disgruntled. Consequently, the meeting had its problems.

Fortunately the Home Mission Board of the Five Years Meeting saw the Friends meeting in the nation's capital as an important one. It helped persuade Murray Kenworthy to go there and assisted some in his meager salary.

Brought up in a partially programmed meeting as a boy and familiar with Friends in unprogrammed meetings through his work with the American Friends Service Committee and in other contacts, Quakers felt that he could understand that approach to worship. He was known, too, as an inspiring speaker, and Friends who yearned for a more acceptable spoken ministry felt he could speak to their condition. In addition, he was respected as a reconciler and nearly all the Irving Street Friends recognized the importance of that talent or cluster of talents.

Eventually a mode of worship was developed which was as satisfying to everyone as human beings could devise. The regular meetings for worship were held on the basis of silence or expectancy and four or five Friends, including Murray Kenworthy, sat on the platform in the front of the room, much as people would on a facing bench. There were no announcements and no collection plate to disturb the atmosphere of worship. Murray always came with a brief, prepared message or sermon. But if the meeting moved in a way in which his prepared message would not fit appropriately, he discarded it, either speaking in the mood of the meeting, or occasionally not at all.

There were hymnals on the benches and a piano at the side of the meeting with someone sitting near it in case anyone called for a hymn. Often, but not always, that occurred, and usually it fit into the worship. Often there were gathered meetings–times of healing, times of adoration and praise, times of seeking, times of renewal and dedication–frequently brought together or focused by Murray's ministry. In talks with members and attenders he sometimes encouraged (and a few times discouraged) Friends to be faithful in the spoken ministry as well as in the use of silence. But it was in the total life of that group that breaches were hurdled, bridges built, the varying needs of a divergent group met, and a feeling of a close-knit family or community fostered.

Sunday evenings there was a Christian Endeavor meeting, with different young people in charge and widespread participation, including singing. The parents were there, too, although they tried to keep in the background.

The First Day School or Sunday School allowed the chance for an evangelical Friend to lead the singing with his booming voice and his trusty baton. In the meeting membership there were few young children, but several boys and girls came from a nearby orphanage for that part of the meeting's activities.

There were two lively classes of younger people. One class of eight to ten boys was taught by Dr. Matthew Woodward, a medical doctor in the Veterans Administration and a Boy Scout worker. The other class was young people of high school and college age. Two of the young men in that group who later became prominent among Friends were Sam Levering and Merrill Hiatt.

Mid-week service was on Wednesday evenings. Murray Kenworthy sometimes lectured, drawing upon his wide knowledge of the Bible, of the history of Christianity and Quakerism, and of world religions. Such sessions served an educational function for the members of that meeting and provided Dad with opportunities for a teaching ministry.

Undergirding those and other activities were the social times together. Some of them were at the Stanton home in Bethesda, Maryland, where some of us played tennis while the older folks talked or worked together. Others were the Flinch card parties in which some Friends indulged and other shunned as merely a Quaker substitute for bridge. Still others were the parties at the meetinghouse, with short programs put on by the members, good food, and sherbert or ice cream made by the younger boys under Dr. Woodward's direction.

As he did everywhere he served as a pastor or minister, Dad did a great deal of visiting with members and attenders, carrying on some of the pastoral duties of the group.

For the young men of the meeting there was a basketball team for a time and at another point a bowling team, master-minded by Omar and Vernon Lee Brown. Murray was the sponsor for both groups, and he seldom missed a practice of the basketball team in the gym of the Wilson Teachers College, or a game. He did not play basketball himself, but he did occasionally bowl with those young men.

Through these activities the Irving Street Meeting members and attenders became a caring community, a lively and loving fellowship, a

Society of Friends. Differences did not all disappear, but they were often forgotten or laid aside. Sometimes they would appear in monthly meetings where Friends would strive for the sense of the meeting without always achieving it. But many of the business meetings were really meetings for worship to do business.

Curiously I remember some of them, including the naming of committees when the full names of appointees would be suggested. When the clerk asked for the names of Friends to be named to a particular committee, they would be called out–even to the middle initial–Rose *L.* Hiatt, Matthew *F.* Woodward, Vernon *L.* Brown, Edwin *F.* Stanton, Murray *S.* Kenworthy, and so on.

After a disastrous fire in the Irving Street Meeting the two meetings met jointly for a few months in the Eye Street meetinghouse. Out of that experience emerged a couple of joint committees, and later the Eye Street Friends asked Murray Kenworthy if he would be willing to serve as joint pastoral secretary of the two groups.

Because Dad's salary was so small, he was released by the meeting for part of the time in order to do other work. For several months he worked part-time with Frederick J. Libby in the National Council for the Prevention of War. His big achievement in that period was the organization of a District of Columbia branch of the NCPW.

In another period he worked with the Federation of Churches of the District of Columbia, organizing a chaplaincy service and performing some of the services of a chaplain in hospitals in Washington. He found that extremely taxing and eventually gave it up.

That work, however, brought him into contact with the ministers of various denominations and he took part in a few joint worship services of the Washington Federation. One especially outstanding one which I recall and for which I still have the program was the Annual Christmas Service, held at the Foundry Methodist Episcopal Church on 16th Street, with Calvin Coolidge, then President of the United States, and his entourage, present. At that service our family was seated in the special section reserved for the President.

Although extremely busy, Dad was continually concerned with the education of his sons. Carroll was in college and Wilmer in Westtown. But for a part of the period in Washington Dad and I lived together. He purchased one ticket for the outstanding lecture series of the National Geographic Society, and we took turns going to it, depending upon the nature of the program. Then, on Sunday evenings, after the Christian Endeavor service in the Irving Street Meeting, we attended various churches. Both before and after those services, he would explain the history of those denominations and their methods of worship.

Unforgettable was the Sunday morning during yearly meeting in Baltimore when we attended an early mass at the Catholic Cathedral and then Dad sat on the facing bench at the Friends Meeting later that day. What a lesson in interdenominational understanding that was for me.

Another lesson in tolerance was the time he took me to the Calvary Baptist Church to hear William Jennings Bryan, the silvertongued orator and the perennial Democratic candidate for president of the United States. That was just before the famous Scopes Trial in Tennessee which pitted William Jennings Bryan against Clarence Darrow on the question of teaching the theory of evolution in the schools of that state. At the time Dad was reading a book by the prominent Harvard geologist Kirtley Mather entitled *The Earth Speaks to Bryan*. It presented the claims of those who believed in evolution. Of course Dad was opposed to Bryan's views, but he felt that I should see and hear this famous individual. And so we went to that lecture.

Meanwhile Dad was corresponding with an old friend and Earlham classmate, Violet Cosand, and seeing her on his rare visits to Indiana. Eventually they became engaged and were married in Indianapolis in 1926. As a wife and mother, Violet helped to fill the void in the life of Murray Kenworthy and his sons. She had been born and brought up in New London, Indiana, and attended school and the Friends Meeting there. In Earlham College she had been a classmate and friend of Lenora Holloway and Murray Kenworthy. In her quiet and characteristic manner, she picked up where her friend Lenora had left off even to the point of finishing the tulip pattern quilt Lenora had started.

After college Violet had taught in New London, Kokomo, and Indianapolis. She was a wonderful teacher of literature and gifted writer of poetry, plays, and pageants. Among the best known and most widely used of her pageants was one written for the tercentenary of George Fox, which was printed in *The American Friend* and produced in several localities.

She was a quiet and friendly person, with the special talent of listening sympathetically to others. She seldom gave advice but always was supportive. Soon she won her way as a friend of everyone in the Irving Street Meeting, as she had done everywhere she had lived prior to that.

The Irving Street Meeting was a small group with no wealthy members. It was a struggle for them to raise Dad's salary, but somehow they raised enough money to give him a new Ford car as a wedding present. So he drove that automobile slowly across the mountains to Indiana and then back again to Washington with Violet Cosand Kenworthy as his new life companion. Surely that gift was a significant symbol of the admiration and affection in which Washington Friends held Murray Kenworthy.

During the years he had been in Washington, Herbert Hoover had occasionally attended the Friends Meeting on Eye Street. But during the 1928 campaign for the presidency (when Hoover was the nominee of the Republican Party), word was circulated that he was a Unitarian because many people associated Hicksite Quakers with that theology. Fearing that that label would harm him, he started going to the small Orthodox Ashton Meeting outside Washington. Occasionally he came to the Irving Street Meeting.

As head of the American and British Quaker relief work in the Soviet Union in 1921 and 1922, Dad had had some contact with Herbert Hoover and was not one of his great admirers. Furthermore, Dad felt that his ministry, especially the social aspects of it, would have to be curbed if the President was present, lest the newspaper reporters interpret his comments as telling the President what to do. Reluctantly, therefore, he submitted his resignation to the Irving Street Monthly Meeting and told Friends in the Eye Street Meeting about his decision to leave.

To take Murray Kenworthy's place, the Hoovers asked their old friend (and Friend) from Stanford University, Augustus Murray, to come to Washington. They contributed most of the additional funds needed to persuade him to accept. He was a professor of Greek and an authority on John Greenleaf Whittier; there was little likelihood that he would be particularly interested in contemporary social issues.

The next few months were difficult for both groups in Washington. They had been growing together gradually, in good Quaker fashion. Now strong pressure was exerted for them to unite quickly and to build a new meetinghouse on Florida Avenue. As a result of that action, there were three groups in the nation's capital for considerable time; some Friends in the Eye Street and Irving Street groups were unwilling to unite. Today the scars of that conflict have disappeared, and the Florida Avenue Meeting is a large and lively one. It has spawned other meetings in the suburbs.

FSC
IN THE
MIDWEST

One of the most significant and heartening developments in American Quakerdom in this century has been the formation and growth of the American Friends Service Committee. Formed in 1917 it concentrated in the first period of its existence on relief work in Europe. Once that effort was largely accomplished, it turned to special activities to foster peace, to improve race relations, and to relieve the miserable conditions of coal miners and others in the U.S.A., caused by the Depression of 1929.

The AFSC, as it is familiarly known, was organized primarily by Friends from unprogrammed meetings, but it included some others from various parts of the U.S.A. In its desire to be an arm of all Friends, it has customarily appointed Quakers from outside Philadelphia to the post of executive secretary. The first person to hold that job was Vincent Nicholson, who lived in the Philadelphia area but was born and raised in Indiana. Its long-time chairman was Rufus Jones, who spent most of his life in the Philadelphia area but was born and raised in Maine. He retained his membership throughout his life in New England Yearly Meeting in order to be a part of the Five Years Meeting, which he had helped to create. The second executive secretary was Wilbur K.

Thomas, who had been born in Indiana but had attended Friends University in Wichita, Kansas. The third secretary was Clarence Pickett, who was born in Illinois, raised in Kansas, and attended William Penn College in Iowa. He was the pastor of the Toronto Meeting in Canada and the Friends Meeting in Oskaloosa, Iowa, and then a professor at Earlham College in Indiana.

As the AFSC grew and matured, it nurtured several innovative programs, such as work camps, peace caravans for young people, and international relations institutes. Then it launched two movements which involved hundreds of Friends in all parts of the United States and from the wide variety of Quakerism in this country. One of them was the formation of sewing groups in private homes and in Friends meetings and the collection drives for clothing to be used abroad or in the United States. Those efforts meant that many people could contribute to the alleviation of distress around the world. The second movement was the establishment of several regional offices for the AFSC, with local committees of Friends in charge of their activities.

The first of those regional offices came as the result of a concern by several Friends in the East Central states that the AFSC involve Quakers more in that area than it had done before. The executive committee which was responsible for the formation of that regional branch was an incredible one: Herschel Folger and Elsie McCoy, Wilmington Yearly Meeting (Orthodox); the C.B. Thomases, Indiana Yearly Meeting (Conservative); Wilson Doan, Marianna Dudley, and C. Merwin Palmer, Indiana Yearly Meeting (Hicksite); B. Willis Beede, Elizabeth and Fred Emerson, Thomas R. Kelly, Elizabeth Marsh, Homer L. Morris, Clarence E. Pickett, Ruthanna M. Simms, Margaret D. Webb, Charles M. Woodman, and Walter C. Woodward, Indiana Yearly Meeting (Orthodox); and Anna and Howard Brinton, Philadelphia Yearly Meeting (Orthodox).

Later, several names were added from Western Yearly Meeting (Orthodox). Five of the committee were on the faculty of Earlham College: the Brintons, Thomas Kelly, Homer Morris, and Clarence Pickett; others were on the staff or active in the work of the Five Years Meeting, such as Elizabeth Marsh, B. Willis Beede, and Walter C. Woodward, the editor of *The American Friend* and the executive secretary of the nation-wide Quaker group.

There was some hesitation at first lest the AFSC office duplicate the work of the Five Years Meeting and detract from the support by middle western Quakers of that organization. But in a series of small meetings those objections to the new regional office were met, and the leaders of the Five Years Meeting gave their whole-hearted support to the extension of the Service Committee in the middle west.

There was unanimous agreement in the planning committee from the start that the first secretary of the Midwest regional office should be Murray S. Kenworthy. After all, he was a Hoosier by birth, had served as a pastor in meetings in Indiana and Western Yearly Meetings, and had been on the faculty of Earlham College. In addition, he had been the executive secretary of Wilmington Yearly Meeting. He had twice been acting head of the AFSC and had visited many meetings in that area during his year as a fundraiser for that organization. He came from the large Orthodox group, but he was nevertheless well-known and highly respected by Friends of other groups in the Midwest as well as in the East.

Again it was Wilbur Thomas who approached Murray Kenworthy, as he had done when he invited him to go to the Soviet Union to administer Quaker relief in that country in 1921-1922. Murray and Violet soon decided that this was an important assignment to which they should give a few years of their lives. So in 1928 they moved to College Avenue in Richmond.

There was considerable criticism of the American Friends Service Committee then by many midwestern Friends who felt it was solely a relief agency like the American Red Cross and therefore not evangelical and proselytizing. Aware of that feeling, Dad made a statement about the AFSC which was undoubtedly circulated widely in that part of the country. It read, in part, as follows:

> In explaining the present situation and plans for the future to those who are in doubt as to the advisability of such efforts, it might be well to make the original purpose of the ASFC clear. When that is done, it should be seen as not just another organization, not just another branch of American Quakerism, but a *joint* commmittee, composed of representatives of the various groups of Friends, empowered to serve the entire Society in activities in which they are all concerned. It is thus a coordinating element–a cement that can bind the various groups, as well as an active agent in carrying on well-known historical concerns.
>
> Of course its period of greatest activity was during and just after the war. Its reason for continuing is not as spectacular but just as real.
>
> When fully understood, there should be no conflict of this

social outreach of the Society with its spiritual life; they should be seen as inseparable, just as there was no conflict in the life of Jesus who could pass from the Mount of Transfiguration to the plains of everyday living, both as expressions of God's witness to the fuller life.

Two provisos were agreed upon for Dad's work. One was that he would be designated at first as a field secretary of the American Friends Service Committee rather than as the director of a regional office. The other was that he would not duplicate the activities of the Five Years Meeting. Those conditions were acceptable to him, and it was soon evident that there was enough work to keep the Five Years Meeting and the AFSC busy without overlapping with each other.

The question then arose as to what one man, without any office staff (even a secretary) could do in a region as large as that of the East Central States. His reports to the Philadelphia office during the next two years reveal how much he was able to accomplish single-handedly.

First, he needed to develop a mailing list of key persons who could receive letters, information bulletins, and appeals for financial aid. Lists from the Philadelphia office were a start. His knowledge of people in the area helped. So did the lists of people in the annual proceedings of the various yearly meetings in the area. To them were added key persons in colleges and in other groups.

Of course he needed to encourage existing monthly meeting peace and service committees, to reactivate those which were not now active, and to urge the formation of others. Then he developed a list of practical suggestions for their work: peace contests to involve young people; circulation of books on peace, race relations, and industrial democracy; preparation of articles for local papers; work with organizations of boys and girls (such as the Scouts); and sponsoring meetings and conferences. Occasionally a committee could develop some special activity which would reach hundreds of people, such as a booth at the Indiana State Fair in Indianapolis. Thus his own work could be multiplied many times by others.

From time to time he could also arrange speaking engagements for leading Friends from abroad or other parts of the United States and for past or present Service Committee workers. Among such distinguished visitors were Henry T. Hodgkin; and Rowntree Gillett from England, and Nevin Sayre of the Fellowship of Reconciliation. An especially intriguing activity he arranged was a program of folk dances and a talk on the Soviet Union by Harry and Rebecca Timbres.

Dad was a very knowledgeable speaker on a wide range of topics, and he made himself available to schools and colleges, service clubs, and women's groups, and Friends meetings. His subjects included "The World War Debts," "The International Court of Justice," "American Exclusion Acts and the Orient," "The American Policy of Isolation," "Uncle Sam and the Caribbean Republics," "The Future of Russia," and "Storm Centers." Soon he was in demand as a speaker, especially in high schools. Frequently he could combine engagements in a community with several groups—a high school in the morning or in the afternoon, a talk to a service club at their noon meeting, and a Quaker group in the evening, often with the public invited. In addition, he attended many yearly and quarterly meetings. He often spoke to the entire group and then sat down for a planning session with the peace or peace and service committee for that body.

Another complicated but rewarding aspect of his work was the scheduling of the Peace Caravans through that region in the summer. These groups of young people were devoting their vacations to representing the AFSC and meeting with Quaker groups and others here and there.

Two urgent problems against which he worked valiantly but unsuccessfully were the incorporation of military training into many schools and the legislating of a teacher's oath by the Indiana State Legislature. Another concern to which he committed considerable time, effort, and energy was the reactivation of the cooperative work of the three Historic Peace Churches—The Church of the Brethren, the Mennonites, and the Quakers. In that connection he was especially grateful for the cooperation of Andrew Cordier, a professor at Manchester College (a Church of the Brethren institution) who later worked in the State Department of the United States and then served as special assistant to Trygve Lie when he became the first Secretary-General of the United Nations.

There were other important events in which he could be helpful, too. One was the application of Margaret Dorland Webb for United States citizenship. She was a member of a prominent Quaker family from England and Canada. She also was the wife of John R. Webb, the pastor of the East Main Street Friends Meeting in Richmond and member of the executive committee of the AFSC regional office.

Her application for citizenship attracted considerable attention because she was a Quaker and a pacifist. The Supreme Court had recently refused citizenship to Rosika Schwimmer, a prominent pacifist, because she had said that she would not bear arms in any war, even though she was not likely as a woman to be asked to do so.

The day that Margaret Webb's application for citizenship came before the local judge was a special event in Richmond. Many members of the American Legion and the Daughters of the American Revolution sat on one side of the courtroom and a large group of Quakers and supporters of the AFSC sat on the other.

With prodding from the judge, several illiterate or near–illiterate immigrants passed their examination on the Constitution and United States history and were granted citizenship. But when Margaret Webb refused to say she would take part in any war that the United States declared, her application for citizenship was denied. The judge did say, however, that he made his ruling largely because of the recent Supreme Court decision in the Rosika Schwimmer case.

Newspapers and radio broadcasters made much of that decision, and although Margaret Webb did not become a citizen of the United States, that situation did provide an opportunity for the Quaker testimony on peace to be spread widely in that area of the United States.

Dad's report on his work in 1929 provides evidence of the strenuous program in which he engaged. It listed the following events for that one year: speaking at eight yearly meetings, fifteen quarterly meetings, forty-seven local meetings, thirty-five high schools and five colleges; taking part in forty-nine sessions of twenty-one committees; and arranging and taking part in nine weekend conferences.

Through such public presentations and small committee meetings, as well as through many private conversations, he was able to allay some of the fears about the American Friends Service Committee and the charges that it was a secular rather than a spiritually-based organization. The fact that he knew the Bible and Christian and Quaker history well, helped fortify his efforts.

For his second year as secretary of the East Central States area office of the AFSC, Dad and Mother moved to her home in New London. In that way some expenses were eliminated, Dad was more centrally located for travel among Friends in western Ohio, Indiana, western Illionois, and southern Michigan, and mother was able to contribute to their home meeting and community. In 1930 Dad and Mother were ready to settle down to service in one locality rather than traveling so widely. They gave up his work with the AFSC and moved to the Friends Meeting in Amboy, Indiana.

The term "pilot project" originated from the practice of having a tugboat or small vessel test the water in a harbor to see if a larger ship could maneuver in that place. In a way, the first regional office of the American Friends Service Committee in Richmond, Indiana, was a pilot project. Because it was successful, that idea was used later on a wide scale and today there are regional offices in several parts of the country, from one in New England to three on the West Coast. Through those regional offices the work of the AFSC and financial support for it has been vastly extended. Hundreds of people work on various committees and take part in other ways in its work. Dad had pioneered in another important aspect of the development of the Religious Society of Friends in the United States. In that job he had been able to combine in a striking and satisfying way his concern for spiritual nourishment and for social outreach.

Amboy
AND
CARTHAGE
INDIANA

The Amboy Friends Meeting was in a small town in Indiana, and it also served several farm families in that community. It was a large and strong meeting which served in some ways as a community church. Therefore, it contained in its fellowship people of a wide variety of theological viewpoints and would call upon all Dad's diplomacy and Christian charity to meet the needs of all the members and attenders. It was not far from New London where Dad's parents and Mother's sister were still living, so it served as a near-ideal place for them to live and work in the next few years.

Those years, from 1930 to 1937, were not always easy for Dad and Mother, but they were enjoyable and rewarding years. They were friendly with everyone and their friendship was reciprocated. Their influence on the meeting and on the community was powerful, especially on an entire generation of young married couples.

Curiously, Willis Kenworthy had moved to Amboy around 1885, becoming its first "donation minister," which meant that he worked part-time as a farmer and received "gifts" in place of a regular salary. Hence Murray was following in the footsteps of his grandfather in some respects. Another coincidence was the fact that Wilbur K. Thomas, the secretary of the American Friends Service Committee who had asked Murray to go to the Soviet Union, was born in Amboy.

The Meeting in Amboy was one of the largest in Indiana Yearly Meeting. After the First Friends Meeting in Richmond and the First Friends Meeting in Muncie, it had the largest attendance of any Quaker group in that area with well over two hundred at Sunday School and an average of 180 at the meeting for worship.

Murray accepted the invitation to teach the young married class in the Sunday School. Sunday after Sunday he spoke briefly at the beginning of the period in order to provide background on the lesson. Then he encouraged comments and questions from as many people as possible. Two goals dominated his teaching: the application of Christianity to daily living and the involvement of as many participants as possible. Probably that aspect of his work in Amboy was the most productive and the most gratifying of all he did there as he helped to educate a generation of future leaders and through them, their children.

Since the Amboy Meeting was in many respects a community church and they were accustomed to a programmed service, he did not change that pattern drastically. But he did attempt to introduce a lengthy period of silence or expectant waiting. Unfortunately, however, it was monopolized by one woman almost every Sunday. Hence the silence never lasted very long and many were perturbed by the woman's highly emotional ministry. Murray was forced to alter that open period slightly, according to the circumstances or the attendance of that one Friend. In the mid-week meeting, however, the smaller group was often able to settle into silent worship better, with occasional brief messages or prayers.

For many members of the Amboy Meeting, Murray's sermons were the highlight of the week. He felt that they came to him largely through his visits with members and attenders, thus making him aware of what messages might be helpful. Frequently he had several themes on which he was working–not just as he sat in his study but as he walked the streets, gardened, worked on his automobile, or took long drives in the car with Mother.

His sermons were on a wide range of themes because different people needed different messages. And since there was such a variety of individuals in the congregation, he tried to have illustrations that would speak to all of them. He often used examples for his main theme which were tailored for farmers, for housewives, for professional people, and for children. Each minister needs to work out ways that are helpful in preparing sermons. Dad had his own special method. He used only one small sheet of paper, 4 3/4 by 7 3/4 in size, with his writing or typing on only one side. In that way he had some notes as a guide to what he would say, but was not held to them; he could speak as the Spirit moved him. There was almost always an introduction and a conclusion, with two to four major points and illustrations. Although he almost always had one central theme, he always used at least one verse from the Bible.

A glance at some of the outlines of his sermons reveals the breadth and practical nature of his messages. Here are a few of the texts from one book of his sermons:

Romans 12:1 Present your bodies a living sacrifice.
Psalm 65:11 Thou art crowning the year with thy goodness.
Acts 22:3 Educated at the feet of Gamaliel. (Moffatt)
Proverbs 23:7 As a man thinketh within himself, so is he.
Habakkuk 3:17-19 Even so...I will rejoice in the Lord.
Luke 24:5 Why do you look among the dead for Him who is alive?
Luke 2:49 Thy father and I have been searching for thee in sore anxiety. (A Father's Day message)
John 10:10 I came that they might have life abundantly.
Exodus 13:18 God led the people.

As indicated by the reference above to "Moffatt," he made much use of the modern translations of Goodspeed, Moffatt, and Weymouth to supplement or complement earlier translations and/or to find language which would be better understood by everyone.

In that period of his life he listened almost every Sunday to the National Vesper Service conducted by Harry Emerson Fosdick. He admired Fosdick greatly because of his beliefs, because of the way in which he withstood the attacks on him as a modernist, and because of his ability to speak cogently and convincingly to the condition of thousands in his radio audience.

Murray also read the many books of Harry Emerson Fosdick, such as *Understanding the Bible, The Meaning of Service,* and *The Meaning of Prayer,* as well as the books of Rufus Jones, George Buttrick, and others, underlining them judiciously.

There were a few local Friends, however, who questioned Murray's theology and urged him to preach "hell, fire, and damnation." Quietly he went to the two most outspoken of his critics and talked with them, but to no avail. Their publicly expressed criticisms hurt Murray Kenworthy deeply, but he never condemned them in public or in private.

At Amboy he continued his pastoral calls, often making them in the evening when the whole family could be present. Despite the size of the Meeting, he was able to visit nearly every family over a period of a few months.

On rare occasions he would raise questions with them about some aspect of their lives. I recall one example he shared with me. It concerned a member who had a magnificent barn and a miserable house. In as persuasive a manner as possible, Murray asked him one time if he realized what that might mean–that he prized his animals far more than his family. Murray was not always successful in such dangerous but important counseling sessions. But in that case the farmer soon added new features to his home including an extension so that his children could each have a room of his or her own.

On another occasion he learned that workmen were repairing the railroad track near Amboy. In that group was a Jamaican who was either a Friend or who knew Quakers in his homeland. It turned out that he was also an accomplished singer. So Dad invited the entire "gang" to the Sunday services and asked the Jamaican to sing a solo. But when Dad looked for an accompanist, two of the pianists turned him down. Fortunately Louise Hoke, a teacher in the winter in Illinois, was home for the summer and gladly accompanied the black man for his solo. A few Friends spoke to Dad afterwards, but that incident did not become a big issue.

Murray and Violet spent a great deal of time, energy, and thought with the large group of young people. Murray held a class for the transfer of young people from associate to adult membership. He and Violet held several parties in the church basement for that group, too. And each year several young people went with the Kenworthys to Quaker Haven, the camp of Indiana and Western Yearly Meetings in northern Indiana. Usually Murray, and sometimes Violet, were not only chaperones but camp counsellors and group discussion leaders.

Murray also encouraged several young people from Amboy to go to college. Nearly all of them went to Earlham. Sometimes their families were clear that that should happen; in other instances the families were hesitant, thinking that they would never return to the Amboy community after they had completed their college education. Among those young people I recall were LuVine Ballard, Lemoine Overman, Jesse Overman, Orville Snyder, Morris Snyder, and a couple of others who were at Earlham only a short time.

There was some criticism that Dad was depriving the local community of these promising young people. But he persisted in his efforts even though he thought deeply about ways of encouraging young people to continue their education and yet not siphon them off from their local communities.

Meanwhile Mother used every conceivable occasion for get-togethers of the young girls, either in the parsonage or in the meetinghouse. There were simple parties for the holidays, with cookies cut in the form of log rails for a Lincoln's birthday party or hearts for Valentine's Day. Often she would write skits or playlets which the girls would read aloud.

Dad did not enjoy writing, but he felt it was another form of outreach. So he began to write more and to print pamphlets or leaflets. They were often produced at a discount by a local Friend, Roy Melton, who was a printer. In such efforts he was given a great deal of help by Mother.

In the Amboy Meeting were many individuals and families who were new to Friends worship. Some of them pressed Murray at times on a few of the Quaker testimonies and beliefs. One such issue was the sacraments, so he wrote a small, eighteen-page leaflet, *Friends and the Sacraments,* which was used locally and then in a much wider area. It was one of the shortest and most readable accounts on a topic about which little had been written in recent years by Friends. In that booklet he repeated the Quaker belief in sacraments: that baptism and communion were inward rather than outward experiences. He cited scriptural passages to support his contentions, because many of the inquirers were biblically-centered Christians.

On the final page of that pamphlet he demonstrated his respect for a variety of points of view, saying:

> In view of the many conflicting doctrinal statements, what should be the Christian attitude? Certainly we cannot call fire down from heaven upon those who differ from us. That would bring a merited rebuke from The Master. Rather let us grant that freedom of conscience which will enable everyone to believe and practice the elements of religion that appeal to him as divine. If his decision favors water baptism, for instance, let him choose that method; if he finds that the teaching of Jesus limits baptism to that of the Holy Spirit, as Friends believe, let him answer to his own conscience and to God.

In those days many high schools in Indiana (and in some other states) had courses on the Bible or on the New Testament as a part of their curriculum. Amboy High School was one of them. For six years Dad taught one or two periods a day in that school. He enjoyed that work, and it gave him further contact with young people. But it was not always easy to give grades to the sons or daughters of meeting members, especially if they were really failing the course!

Meanwhile he kept up his work on various committees of Indiana Yearly Meeting and the Five Years Meeting–on peace, Indian affairs, temperance, education, and missions. He missed contact with ministers of other denominations, so he went to Kokomo or Marion from time to time to attend the luncheons of the ministerial associations. There he cultivated his friendships with some of those men (and they were all men at that time) and exchanged ideas and experiences.

In 1937 Dad was selected as the executive secretary of Indiana Yearly Meeting. He resigned his pastorate at Amboy and was ready to assume that important post. Then a small but vocal group of extreme fundamentalists attacked that appointment so bitterly that the committee in charge relented and reconsidered, asking Murray to step aside.

Asked recently to comment on their memories of Dad in Amboy, several individuals responded, despite the fact that that was about fifty years ago. Dale and Lola Prout, who have served the Amboy meeting many years as clerk and as treasurer as well as in other assignments, remembered him as "one of our most thoughtful, outstanding, and best-liked ministers, with lots of practical advice for young couples." Another said, "We have had many pastors here over the years but Murray Kenworthy's name leads the list."

Glennis Douglas, a clerk for several years, recalled the importance to their children of the booklet on membership which Dad wrote when they were adolescents and recalled him "as a practical Quaker and Christian, a good sermonizer, and one who conducted the worship in a spiritual and dignified manner. He was an intellectual speaker, and I remember we always had something to take home with us to try to practice."

Jeanette McKeefer recalled how frequently he visited all the members, attenders, and others: "He was a gentle, dignified man who was constantly reading and seeking knowledge. He was especially interested in the work of the American Friends Service Committee and in world affairs."

The Gordons remembered how frequently he was a comfort to members of families, including theirs, when there were deaths or other troubles.

Because of their admiration for Murray Kenworthy, Laurel and Helen Gordon Vincent named their third child Murray Vincent. Such was the affection with which Amboy Friends held their long-time pastor.

Dad often said that a pastor should not stay in one place for more than five years because no one person could meet the needs of all the members of a meeting. A quite different pastor probably should be chosen as a successor. Thus, if a minister was a good preacher and not as adept as a pastor, he might well be followed by one who was a good pastor but not necessarily a good preacher. My own judgement is that he and Mother had more impact in Amboy than in some other places because they stayed more than five years. But different circumstances may alter that advice.

Just at this unsettled point in their lives, the Friends meeting in Carthage was looking for a pastor. Cecil Haworth was leaving, after only a year there, to move to the large High Point Meeting in North Carolina. Realizing that Murray Kenworthy might be available, they contacted him and pled with him and Violet to come to Carthage.

Dad was 63 at that time and it seemed reasonable for him to take a pastorate with a smaller group of Quakers rather than with a large city congregation. Carthage was close to Richmond, and that would make it possible for him to continue his active part in committees and boards of the Five Years Meeting. It was not too far from New London where his parents and mother's sister were living. And it was a community with a long and outstanding record as a Quaker stronghold. Dad and Mother were glad to accept the call from the Carthage Friends Meeting and to move there in 1937 to stay for the next five years.

At that juncture Carthage was beginning to think about its centennial celebration. One of Dad's first jobs was to do a great deal of research on the history of that meeting for a booklet. Like so many Indiana Friends meetings, Carthage drew its original settlers from North Carolina, from Ohio, from other parts of Indiana, and a few from Pennsylvania. Tracing its history back like a genealogical record, Dad discovered that it had its roots in the Westland Monthly Meeting in Fayette County, Pennsylvania.

The early settlers first established the Walnut Ridge Meeting near Carthage. In 1839 Carthage was set off as a preparative meeting. At that time three committees were formed. They were for the care of the poor, for Indian rights, and for "people of color"–a reference to Negroes (or blacks) and the Underground Railroad. In those years between the establishment of the Carthage Preparative Meeting and the Civil War, several local Friends were active in the Underground Railroad, making their homes "stations" on that famous road to freedom. Contrary to what happened in other communities, some of the Negroes stayed in Carthage. After the Civil War, Friends in Carthage were active supporters of the Freedmens Bureau of Indiana Yearly Meeting which assisted with the education of Negroes in the south and in their economic adjustment to freedom.

As early as 1840 a First Day School was established in the Carthage Meeting. Just before the turn of the century they organized a Christian Endeavor Society. Meanwhile many members supported such Quaker concerns as peace, temperance, Indian rights, and education (including an interest in Earlham College).

Like other Quaker meetings, Carthage eventually adopted the pastoral system; its first paid minister was Alpheus Trueblood in 1899. Another feature of that meeting and community was the development of a Friends library which was given to the town in 1890 as a basis for its free public library.

Even though the revival movement took hold in some of the meetings in what became Walnut Ridge Quarter, it never became a predominant feature of the Carthage group. And since there were other Protestant churches in Carthage at the time Dad and Mother were there, the meeting was less of a community church and more of a Friends meeting.

Throughout its history certain families were prominent in the meeting, among them the Binfords, Coffins, Hadleys, Henleys, Hunts, Jessups, Newbys, Parkers, Pickerings, Thornburgs, Wellses, Winslows, and many others.

Dad was uneasy about the lack of young people in the meeting and saddened by the fact that so many of them had moved to Richmond, Indianapolis, Chicago, Cincinnati, or elsewhere. Some such movement was to be expected as farms became more mechanized and larger and the national economy more industrial. But he thought that some special efforts could be made to hold some of the younger people on the farms and in small towns like Carthage. His concern on that subject led, later, to the formation of the Rural Life Association.

On a smaller scale, his activities and those of Mother were similar to the work they had carried on in Amboy: sermons, study groups, Sunday School teaching, pastoral calls, counseling, committee meetings, and social affairs. He did not, however, teach in the local school as he had in Amboy.

After the death of Dad's stepmother, Milton Kenworthy tried to live alone in New London for a short time. That was an unsatisfactory arrangement, and he moved to Carthage to live with Murray and Violet. Being uprooted after a long life in one community was unsettling, but he adjusted to it admirably. He could not bring his horse or cow, but he did bring some chickens and several hives of bees, which pleased him. Soon, however, he had severe difficulty with one leg, and finally had to

100

have it amputated at the knee. In the weeks that followed, Dad did most of the "nursing" of his father, spelled from time to time by Charles Winslow, an elderly Friend in Carthage who was a recorded minister. Murray was eternally grateful to him for that special aid and spoke of it frequently in the following years.

In 1939 Carthage Friends Meeting held its centennial celebration, based on the date of its establishment as a Preparative Meeting. As mentioned already, Dad's written history of that Meeting was complemented by Mother's series of short plays depicting some of the major activities of Friends over that long period. The three most recent pastors of the Carthage Friends Meeting were still able to take part in that series of special services. They were Nathan Pickett, James Furbay, and Cecil Haworth.

In April of 1942, Walter C. Woodward, long-time editor of *The American Friend* (now *Quaker Life*) died. The editorial board was at a loss as to what to do! He had long been almost a one-man staff, as well as serving as General Secretary of the Five Years Meeting (now Friends United Meeting).

With Murray Kenworthy in nearby Carthage, they felt he could fill that position part-time for a few weeks while they decided upon the new editor. Dad agreed to "pinch-hit," and the Carthage meeting released him for half-time work in Richmond. Since the editorial board did not find a successor for eight months, Dad continued for all that time.

INDIANA YEARLY MEETING

In 1942 Friends in Indiana Yearly Meeting again approached Murray Kenworthy to serve as their executive secretary. In the intervening years since they had named him to that post and then had withdrawn their appointment, much had occurred. The yearly meeting had continued to decline drastically in membership and it was wracked with problems. The committee responsible for finding someone for that position agreed that there was no one else with Dad's qualifications. They were determined this time to secure his services. They did not expect him, single-handed, to solve all their problems (or did they?), but they felt certain that he could do much to analyze their dismal situation and to start working on solutions.

In 1937 it had been relatively easy for Dad and Mother to say yes to the invitation of Indiana Yearly Meeting. This time it was more difficult for them to decide what to do. Dad was now 68, and many people were retiring at 65. Indiana Yearly Meeting was very large and geographically widespread, even including a quarterly meeting in the state of Washington. That meant his work would involve much travel, made more difficult by the gas rationing of World War II. The yearly meeting was also plagued with problems—from the decline of the rural and small-town meetings to theological differences.

For some time Dad and Mother had looked forward to retirement in their home community of New London. After all, their three sons were well-established, and their own parents were no longer living, so they had no responsibility in that area. How easy it would be to retire! How comfortable! How enjoyable!

But they were not the kind of people who made their decisions on the basis of how it would affect their personal comfort. They realized that there was much to be done and that Dad had many qualifications for that job. He was a Biblical scholar, even though some of his interpretations of that book did not please some Quakers. He knew church history and the story of Quakerism extremely well. He had been a pastor in several places in Indiana over his long life, including Amboy and Carthage very recently–both in Indiana Yearly Meeting. His committee work and his activities as secretary of the Midwest regional office of the AFSC had taken him into most of the meetings of the yearly meeting. In addition, he had served in a similar post in Wilmington Yearly Meeting and thereby was acquainted with the potentialities as well as the problems of an executive secretary of a yearly meeting. He knew Earlham College well and had participated in conferences at Quaker Haven–both of them owned jointly by Indiana and Western Yearly Meetings. He was acquainted with almost all groups of Quakers in the United States and with their organizations. And despite his liberal views, he was known and respected by almost everyone as a reconciler and bridge-builder between various groups of Quakers. Perhaps, too, there was some feeling on his part that he could still carry out in those later years some of the plans and projects which he had hoped to accomplish back in 1937.

Fortunately he had been blessed all his life with robust health and abundant energy. He had taken care of himself physically and his store of energy had been fed by his devotional life, his clear convictions, and his sense of direction. Consulting a doctor, Dad was told that he was in excellent condition physically, so that possible road block was removed. The Carthage Friends Meeting reluctantly released him from work there. Meanwhile the hard core of opponents to his appointment back in 1937 had dwindled to one or two. Two had died, two had moved into holiness churches outside the Society of Friends, and the others had ceased to be as active in the yearly meeting as they had been before.

Thus the way was clear for Dad to accept the appointment as executive secretary of Indiana Yearly Meeting, with the support of Mother. There was only one proviso: that he would continue his part-time work as acting editor of *The American Friend* until the committee to name a successor to Walter C. Woodward found the right person for that important job.

Believing that it would be best to live near the center of the yearly meeting, Dad and Mother moved to Fairmount, Indiana. That location had another advantage; it was closer to New London than Richmond would have been. Furthermore, it would be a little less expensive than a city like Richmond or Muncie.

When Dad began this new assignment, Indiana Yearly Meeting was the largest group of Quakers in the United States, with approximately fifteen thousand members in ninety-six meetings. (Since that time it has been replaced by North Carolina Yearly Meeting as the largest and the reunited Philadelphia Yearly Meeting as the next largest.) It included Meetings in Indiana, western Ohio, southern Michigan, and a quarterly meeting in the state of Washington.

Over the years Indiana Yearly Meeting had set off four other yearly meetings either directly or indirectly–Western in 1859, Iowa in 1863, Kansas in 1872, and Wilmington in 1892. Thus Richmond played a similar role in the middle west to that of Philadelphia in the east. Furthermore, Richmond was the headquarters of the largest body of Quakers in the world–the Five Years Meeting.

Starting in 1896 and continuing until 1914, the membership of Indiana Yearly Meeting hovered around twenty thousand with as many as 115 Meetings. Then the decline began, with less than fifteen thousand members in 1942. In that year alone there was a loss of more than seven hundred members. (That decline has continued until the present, with less than ten thousand members in the 1980s).

One obvious reason for the precipitous decline was the increase in the size of farms and the mechanization of farming. Thus fewer farmers were needed in Indiana, as elsewhere. At the same time that this "push" was driving farmers off the land, a parallel "pull" was attracting them to the cities. When those people moved to the larger towns, they usually joined a nearby church; they found such places of worship little different from their former meetings. In some ways the city churches offered more–larger and better choirs, better preaching, and more activities–especially for the children and young people. It was reported that at one time there were five thousand Quakers or former Quakers in Chicago, but only one hundred or so of them still were associated with Friends.

Added to population shifts was the decline in the size of families. Thus most Quaker families, like others in that area and time, usually consisted of three or four children rather than six or more. Furthermore, the practice of "birthright" members often inflated the membership roles by adding members who later were not active in Quaker meetings.

Eventually some of them were dropped from the rolls. Still another factor which helps explain the dwindling number of Friends was the fact that highly emotional revival meetings often brought in a good many new members. Frequently they stayed for a few months or years and then either became inactive or moved on to religious groups with a more emotional approach to religion.

A study of the statistical reports for Indiana Yearly Meeting in the early 1940s reveals how much that group was concentrated in small towns and rural areas. Of the ninety-six meetings, more than thirty were rural, another twenty were in towns with less than one thousand population, a little over more than thirty in towns over one thousand. Only five or six were in cities. A further study of the average attendance at the worship services on Sunday morning shows that there were only eight meetings with more than one hundred present (First Friends in Richmond, 225; Muncie, 220; Amboy, 180; Marion, 175; South Marion, 161; Spiceland, 124; New Castle, 120; and Fairmount, 112).

Of the ninety-six meetings in Indiana Yearly Meeting at that time, thirty-three had less than thirty in attendance. That small a group is certainly possible and sometimes desirable in an unprogrammed meeting. But for a programmed meeting it is very small, especially if there is a pastor to be paid. Furthermore, such a group is not likely to provide enough young people for a Christian Endeavor Society or youth group of any kind, and it makes the organization of Sunday School classes extremely difficult, forcing a meeting to have classes that are very small or ones with a wide range in ages.

Murray Kenworthy's chief concern at first was with the situation in small meetings. He recognized that the large Quaker groups had pastors and would not need as much help. Among the tasks that he undertook were the following:

1. To conduct surveys of their present situation and what might be done to improve it.
2. To encourage groups of small meetings to form one congregation.
3. To urge two or three small meetings to hire a pastor jointly.
4. To advocate the purchase by one or more meetings of a parsonage and a few acres to supplement the minister's salary.
5. To promote the sale of available farmland to Quaker couples, thus encouraging them to remain in a given community.

6. To develop local leadership so as not to rely so much on the pastor.
7. To examine the programs of meetings as to their relevancy in the lives of members and attenders and to build new facilities in the present structure or add to it in order to make such much-needed programs possible.
8. To invite Friends from nearby meetings to the local group, and to make sure that the local members and attenders had some contacts with other bodies of Quakers.

Occasionally he had some success with one or two of those suggestions, especially on the idea of local surveys. But he had little luck on most of the others, practical as they were. That was especially true of the idea of uniting two or three small meetings within easy driving distance of each other. People understandably loved the idea of their own community meeting and they were reluctant to even think about amalgamating with other groups. They almost always fought that idea vigorously; they would rather die than unite!

In order to promote a rigorous look at the problems of rural and small-town meetings and to encourage them to take measures which might assure their survival, Dad persuaded the yearly meeting to form a Rural Life Committee.

Their first task was to print a booklet on *The Rural Church in Indiana Yearly Meeting,* written by Murray Kenworthy. It was sold for ten cents or given away to promote its wide use. The book contained an account of the rapidly dwindling membership of Indiana Yearly Meeting, asserting that the decline in rural and small-town meetings was "probably the greatest factor in the lengthening list of causes responsible for our losses." It told, too, about the work of other denominations, such as the efforts of the Presbyterians and Catholics, on this problem. And it raised questions about some of the possible solutions.

But Murray Kenworthy went even further in the booklet than he had usually done publicly, raising the question as to whether the type of evangelist services held in some meetings really aided those groups in the long run. He wrote:

A survey of the statistical reports and a study of current practices and their results, shows that regardless of the type of revival meetings being held, the meetings holding them continue to report losses. Those holding the most fervent type, the so-called "holiness" type, are losing just as heavily in percentage as those which are more "conservative" or even those that seldom or never use the mass type of evangelism.

Such comments were probably like waving a red flag in front of a bull, but he had the facts to prove his point. When asked to expand or expound upon that statement, he pointed out that what happened so often after a revival was that people began to nitpick about theological points, with a subsequent split in the meeting and disastrous decline in attendance and/or membership.

Dad realized that his comments would produce considerable dissent. But he felt it was time that Indiana Quakers (and some elsewhere) faced up to the facts of life and quit claiming that "all that is needed for renewal in our meeting is a series of emotional revival meetings."

In order to concentrate on the problems of rural and small-town communities and Friends meetings, he assisted in the formation of the Rural Life Association, detached from the yearly meeting so that it could act more speedily. Stanley Hamilton, a much-admired and judicious Friend, was selected as its executive secretary; Dad as its chairman. For a while the association performed a useful service; then it was discontinued, largely for a lack of funds.

Murray Kenworthy also was interested in the strengthening of meetings in the larger cities and in the establishment of Quaker groups in large urban areas where none had existed. Everyone agreed that that was a fine idea, but the funds and personnel were not to be found to put the foundations under such a plan, except, perhaps, in Dayton, Ohio. Probably that was a more promising measure than the salvaging of the rural and small-town groups. Their decline, and in some cases death, was inevitable, given the changing demographic pattern of the United States.

Coupled with his concern for the small meeting was his desire to help the many pastors of the yearly meeting. Dad admired many of them and identified closely with nearly all of them. But he was troubled that they were so overworked, so underpaid, and in many cases so poorly prepared for the tasks they were trying so valiantly to accomplish. On that last point he wrote in the booklet on *The Rural Church in Indiana Yearly Meeting* that at least a third of the pastors in that region had no more than a high school education.

Dad realized that George Fox was right that being trained in Oxford or Cambridge did not make one "a man of God," but he knew, too, how well-educated William Penn, Robert Barclay, and Isaac Penington were . He pointed out that George Fox had assembled a large personal library before he died. To Dad education should not make people less spiritual;

it should assist them in the work to which they brought such commitment.

In that area of work he repeated for the most part, but on a larger scale, what he had done in Wilmington Yearly Meeting:

1. To assist in the placement of pastors where they could work most effectively.
2. To persuade meetings to consider seriously women as pastors as women were extremely difficult to place despite the much vaunted equality of men and women in Quakerdom.
3. To develop a course of study for recorded ministers–solely or primarily on their own, where necessary.
4. To encourage gifted and concerned Friends to become full-time or part-time pastors.
5. To visit students in the colleges of the area who were preparing for the ministry or might do so.
6. To hold one-day conferences for ministers (and separate meetings for the spouses of ministers).
7. To counsel with pastors privately when they came to him or wrote him for advice.
8. To press for the establishment in Indiana Yearly Meeting of a pension fund for ministers and missionaries.
9. To urge meetings to increase the remuneration to pastors. Many of them were paid less than the hired hands on farms or clerks in stores.
10. To assist pastors in their preparation of sermons, especially through the one-day conferences already mentioned and through longer periods at Quaker Haven.
11. To bring into the yearly meeting prominent Friends and religious leaders of other denominations who could "speak to the condition" of local pastors.
12. To share with younger pastors, especially, his experience on some practical aspects of their lives.

Perhaps a few brief comments on some of those points are in order here. On several problems he was able to make substantial progress and on others, some improvements. But on a few he was not successful.

He was able to reactivate the yearly meeting committee on the training of those being considered for "recording" of their gifts for ministry. A new course study was developed which included reading and study of and about the Bible, about the history of Christianity, and about the history, beliefs, and practice of Friends. Upon the completion of that course of study, the persons being considered for recording met with members of that review committee, and a recommendation about their recording was made–either for, against, or suggesting further study.

He also was able to work with the ministers on sermon building. He conducted several sessions in the Pastors Short Course, held for five or six days each summer at Quaker Haven. Tacking large sheets of brown paper to a tree or to the wall of the main lodge, Dad would develop two or three different approaches to a text or theme.

That was a practical help to many ministers, and they often expressed their appreciation to Dad. I recall sitting in on some of those sessions one summer when I was waiting tables for that course. On our return trip to Fairmount, I commented that those sermons would probably be preached in fifty Meetings the next Sunday. Dad smiled and said quietly, "At least."

Dad's files were filled with letters from ministers in Indiana Yearly Meeting–some about transfers, some about meeting problems, and some about personal difficulties. As I cleared out those files after Dad's death, I thought they would make a wonderful case study book for the Earlham School of Religion. But even with judicious editing, they really should not be published, so they were burned.

A couple of curious comments have been made to me upon several occasions by ministers who were relatively young when Dad was secretary of Indiana Yearly Meeting regarding the very practical suggestions he occasionally made to them. They recalled, for example, that he urged them not to purchase a car until they had the money for it, so as not to waste money on the interest needed for a loan. Apparently he told more than one person to purchase a good suit and to take it off on Sunday as soon as they got home. He also urged them to purchase good, solid furniture which would last for years rather than pieces which would be shoddy in a short time. He also warned them that unless they made special provision for time off, preferably away from home where no one could reach them, theirs would be a seven day a week, twenty-four-hour-a-day job. And on all these points Murray practiced what he preached.

He was able to get a pension fund started for retired pastors and former missionaries. It was miniscule, but it was a start. For the pastors and for others, he was able to persuade several nationally known Friends to come to the yearly meeting session or special conferences held from time to time. Among those noted in Dad's reports to the yearly meeting on his stewardship of his secretarial responsibilities

Typical Sermon Notes of Murray Kenworthy

Genesis 1:28 and subdue it:and have dominion over it
2:15 God took the man and put him in the garden of
Eden to dress it and keep it   /of God
I Corinthians 10:31 Whatsoever ye do,do all the the Glory

I.Introduction - Cooperating with God - A great Commission
Friends conceive Christian life Spiritual Relation to
God and a Way of Life
These three texts bear directly on importance of above
II.Stewardship of the Whole of Life
1.As the Biblical writer presents it.
   a.Scene in Eden -graphic,beautiful,God;then man in Eden
      turns Eden over to man - now see what you can do.
   b.Vision of Jesus - ox yokes,furniture - Paul good tents
2.Catalogue of things available to us - our garden
   a.Minerals - iron,copper,aluminum oil etc
   b.Fruits,grains,vegetables fibers,woods
   c.Animals,for work or food   1080 in County Evidence
   d.Laws (physics) by which make gadgets,chemicals   February 1946 page 53
   e.Plant food in the soil,air,possible development
3.We also can lose our garden God sent him forth
   from the garden of Eden. 3:23.
   a.Waste of materials - certain animals,birds gone
   b.How long before certain minerals - iron,oil
   c.Soil erosion,leaching - abandoned farms
4.Picture what could be as we cooperate with God
   a.Well kept farm -"mine" only for life-time
   b.Consider "my" property as aid to assignment in life
   c.Conserve farm for local Church members - church live
   d.Set example for younger generation so want farm
   e.Make Church and home grounds beautiful,attractive
III. Cultivate the Spiritual Garden
   a.A first hand,spiritual relation with God
   b.Growth in Grace,knowledge,service
   c.Christianity only can save a frightened atomic world
IV. Conclusion
   Appeal - We people of the rural Churchshould become more
      conscious of our great heritage _of all people we are as
      close or closer to the vast variety of things in God's
      garden

110

were Rufus Jones, William O. Mendenhall–(at that time President of Whittier College in California), Alexander Purdy of the Hartford Theological Seminary, and A.J. Muste (a Friend who was for many years the executive secretary of the interdenominational pacifist group, Fellowship of Reconciliation).

He was troubled that so many of the ministers were studying in non-Friends colleges and were being exposed to teachers who were often highly evangelistic in their approach. But he saw little that he could do about that except to occasionally visit the current ministers and prospective Friends ministers in those institutions. (How Dad would have welcomed the establishment of the Earlham School of Religion in 1963, to which his family gave his splendid collection of sermon notes and many books.) On such points as the wider use of women as pastors and increases in the salaries of pastors he made little progress.

Another area in which Dad tried to concentrate his efforts was the education of young people in the history, beliefs, and practices of Friends. He did not limit that phase of his work to young people, but he did highlight that work with them. He and Mother spent some time each summer at Quaker Haven at the young peoples conferences, as well as at the pastors' short course. Both of them served as counsellors and group discussion leaders and Murray usually gave a series of lectures or presentations, often on Quakerism.

Realizing that he could never touch hundreds of adolescents personally, he worked on a revision of the fifty-three page booklet on *A Preparation Course for Membership with Friends* which he had written when he was in Amboy, and which had been authorized by Indiana Yearly Meeting. It would be used with scores or even hundreds of young people in the coming years, and sometimes with adults.

Sensing the need for a short, semi-popular account of the Religious Society of Friends, he also wrote a fifteen-page booklet on *What Is Quakerism?* Three excerpts from it may suggest the tone of that leaflet and the style in which it was written. Writing about George Fox and the early Friends, he said:

Like a prospector who had found a long-lost gold-bearing lode, Friends felt that they had rediscovered that spiritual vein which characterized the life and activities of the first Christians.

Commenting on the centrality of "experience" in the lives of Friends, he wrote:

As a lover knows the emotions of love, so only those who have had this spiritual rebirth can know its thrill.

Developing the idea of "experience" and the difficulty Friends have had in describing it, he observed that:

No Friend, no writer, however spiritually discerning, has phrased a satisfactory definition. Life-deep, vibrant, vigorous spiritual life of this type is beyond definition.

To those who asked why it is necessary to worship in groups when one can worship alone, he replied:

For these reasons Friends early discovered that there was more light, clearer understanding, and greater strength for service in the spiritually-led group than in the average individual alone.

On the importance of unplanned periods in Quaker worship he comented:

Any Friends Meeting for Worship which makes no provision for the free individual expression of its worshippers is a definite departure from the conception of group worship by early Friends.

Murray Kenworthy was a proponent of the social gospel for most of his life, certainly after his studies with Walter Rauschenbusch at the Harvard Divinity School. He considered spiritual concern and social action inseparable in the life of a Christian–like the two sides of a door, the two sides of a coin.

Largely because of his work in the Soviet Union and his visits to many meetings after that year, and in the period in which he headed the regional office of the American Friends Service Committee in the Midwest, Friends were aware of his commitment to a variety of causes, organizations, and movements. Sometimes he spoke directly on peace, missions, temperance, race relations, and employer-employee relations. More often he cited in his sermons and other messages specific ways of attempting to lead God-directed lives and to bring the Kingdom of God a little closer to fruition here on earth. In that regard he was as much aware of local and state problems as of national and international ones.

Close to his heart was the need for easing tension between modernists and fundamentalists, between liberals and conservatives, and between various aggregations of Friends–such as the Five Years Meeting and the Friends General Conference (at that time composed solely of Hicksite Friends). He did not make speeches or write articles about the differences between groups. Instead he conducted what might be called "quiet diplomacy," talking with individuals and small groups about their dislike of persons with differing beliefs or practices. In that way he hoped to bridge some of the chasms that existed then (and still exist on a smaller scale) between different interpretations of Christianity and of Quakerism.

However, if the occasion seemed to call for the public statement, he would speak out calmly but with conviction. One such occasion was at Indiana Yearly Meeting shortly after the United States entered World War II. Led by William Dennis, the President of Earlham College, a sizeable and articulate group of Friends came dangerously close to asking the yearly meeting to support the war. This perturbed Dad greatly, and he spoke with strong emotions on the floor of the meeting. An impasse developed, but by sitting down together, Dennis and he finally agreed upon a statement which pleased neither of them. It did represent, however, the only compromise possible between their strong points of view. That situation was discovered by the newspapers and the national news magazines. *Time* claimed that for the first time in their long history Quakers had supported a war. That pained Dad, the more so because of his personal friendship of many years with William Dennis.

How did Dad juggle all these important but varied concerns and jobs? He was energetic and healthy. He was well-organized. He looked upon each day as an adventure with God, and upon every contact, committee meeting, conference, and worship service as an opportunity to spread The Good News. Indiana Yearly Meeting was not turned around in his time or by his efforts. But an amazing number of activities were undertaken and some carried to fruition under his leadership. He had done all he could and was only sad that he could not have done more.

To 'DRESS AND KEEP' THE GARDEN

All of Murray Kenworthy's efforts among Friends were based on his belief that people are placed on this planet to develop to their full potential, under God's guidance, and to help to create a better world for everyone. Those twin purposes were to him the essence of Christianity and therefore of Quakerism. A favorite text of his was from Genesis 2:15: "...and God took the man and put him into the Garden of Eden to dress it and keep it." To Dad our globe was still the Garden of Eden and we were still given a mandate by God "to dress it and tend it."

Murray Kenworthy's faith led him to a broad range of concerns. The list of committees, commissions, and boards on which he served in local meetings, quarterly meetings, yearly meetings, Five Years Meeting, and in such organizations as the American Friends Service Committee, the Associated Committee of Friends on Indian Affairs, and the Friends Committee on National Legislation, reflect these concerns. I will include some of the most important of them.

Five Years Meeting. The Five Years Meeting was formed in 1902 and included Baltimore, California, Canada, Indiana, Iowa, Kansas, New England, New York, North Carolina, Oregon, Western, and Wilmington Yearly Meetings. Several years later Kansas and Oregon withdrew over matters of doctrine, but other yearly meetings joined, including Cuba, East Africa, and Jamaica.

Although Dad was the youngest delegate at the meeting in 1902 at which the Five Years Meeting was formed, he was made chairman of the Western Yearly Meeting group. Just why he should have been selected is not known–perhaps to let the youngest member worry about all the details which were demanded of that delegation! From that time on he was present at all or nearly all of the meetings of that national and later international body. He served on many of its committees, commission, and boards.

Education. Murray Kenworthy was closely associated with several of the educational institutions of Friends. He, Lenora, and Violet were all graduates of Earlham College in the class of 1900. Two of his sons graduated from Westtown and one from Oakwood. In addition, his three sons and three grandsons attended Earlham. Dad taught at Wilmington and Earlham, but he was never on the board of any Quaker school or college.

One story may be sufficient to illustrate his concern for Quaker education. During the Depression of 1929 and the years following, Earlham was hard-pressed financially. Yet, despite his small salary and the fact that one son was still in college there, Murray sent a check for fifty dollars–a sizeable contribution in those days. William Dennis told me that story several times with appreciation, saying it showed Murray Kenworthy's devotion to Quaker education in general and to Earlham in particular.

Temperance and Some Puritan Tendencies. If Murray had strong feelings on any topic, it may have been on temperance. That was probably because he had spent so many Saturday evenings at the requests of meeting members in bars trying to persuade their husbands or boy friends to return with him to their homes. Because of those experiences, he was ardent in his espousal of prohibition. However, he was not, to my knowledge, officially connected with the Anti-Saloon League or any other such organizations as were so many Friends in his day. His temperance stand was a part of a general pattern of Puritanism which characterized Quakers in the midwest in those days. Although he was a liberal on religious, political, social, and economic issues, he was a Puritan about card-playing, dancing, and any form of drinking.

Missions. For much of his life Dad was a member of the Foreign Mission Board of Five Years Meeting. For several years he was chairman of its personnel committee and at one time the acting secretary of the Board.

Again, one illustration may suffice to show his attitude towards missionaries and mission work. In the early 1930s a Kansas couple applied for work in Kenya under the American Board of Foreign Missions. They were extrememly well qualified; he was a doctor and she was a nurse. But Kansas Yearly Meeting felt that they were "unsound" theologically, and threatened to withdraw from Five Years Meeting if the couple was appointed. When Dad told me that he and others were likely to send them despite the protest of Kansas Yearly Meeting, I was astounded and asked why he would be a party to such a probable separation among Quakers. His calm but firm reply was that the Mission Board seldom found such qualified people, and that if Kansas did not withdraw over their appointment, they would find some other reason for withdrawal. So the couple went to Kenya and performed a great service there for years. And within a relatively short time Kansas Yearly Meeting withdrew from the Five Years Meeting because of doctrinal differences with it.

Peace. Of all of Murray's concerns peace probably had the highest priority. But his was not just a negative approach, refusing to take part in war or urging others to do the same. His approach was positive, trying to create a climate of opinion for peace, to help construct international institutions which would promote it, and to help build the kind of world in which it could thrive.

Murray's testimony against war and all forms of violence and his positive program for peace was religiously based. He considered Jesus to be the world's greatest advocate of pacifism. That belief of Murray's was supported by the pronouncements of the Religious Society of Friends from almost the beginning of the Quaker movement. Further, he based his opposition to war on economic grounds, pointing to the widespread destruction of lives, property, and even the social and economic fabric of nations. Probably his year in the Soviet Union confirmed his attitude on these points, for he witnessed there the disastrous results of war and revolution.

He worked untiringly in several Quaker and Quaker-allied organizations promoting peace. He was active in the Peace Section of the American Friends Service Committee, in the National Council for the Prevention of War, and in the Peace Association of Friends in America. In addition he cooperated with the Historic Peace Churches and served as the director of the first camp for conscientious objectors in the United States. When World War II arrived, he was active in his support of the Civilian Public Service camps run by Friends, visiting at least two of them (in Indiana and in Maryland) and giving generously to that program.

Cooperation Among Quaker Groups. In a very quiet way Dad tried to build bridges between the various Quaker groups at a time when that was not a very popular concern in many quarters. Eventually he came to know personally many Quakers in the different branches of the Religious Society of Friends in the United States, and he used every possible opportunity to explain their differing points of view to each other.

In Washington, in his activities with the American Friends Service Committee, and in other situaions, he worked closely with members of almost every branch of Quakerism in the United States. Perhaps the most effective bridge he helped to build was in establishing the regional office of the AFSC in the Midwest.

One of the conferences to which he sometimes referred was the All Friends Conference, held in Oskaloosa, Iowa in 1929, called by the American Friends Service Committee. He attended that meeting and often said it was a highlight of his life. He was well aware that unity was not likely to be achieved in his lifetime. He felt that more understanding and more cooperation could be accomplished, however, and he was determined to do what he could to promote such a situation. One of his favorite characterizations of American Quakerdom was expressed by Walter C. Woodward, the long-time editor of *The American Friend*. In a pithy comment he had written, "What a flat and uninteresting landscape would result from uniformity in the Quaker topography."

The World Wide Society of Friends. In 1920 Dad was one of the delegates to the First World Conference of Friends, held in England. That was a glorious experience for him, and it was one of the earliest eye-openers to the wider world about which he learned so much in subsequent years.

Then, at the Second World Conference of Friends, held at Swarthmore and Haverford Colleges outside Philadelphia in 1937, he was again a delegate. At that meeting he had the special joy of having me as a delegate. And Dad's father attended some sessions, although he was not a delegate. Thus three generations of Kenworthys were present at that historic gathering at which the Friends World Commitee for Consultation was formed to foster the world-wide Quaker family.

His Interdenominational Interests. Dad was not interested solely in promoting greater understanding in the Religious Society of Friends. He was interested in interdenominational cooperation. Reference has been made to his part-time work with the Federation of Churches in the District of Columbia, and to his work with the Historic Peace Churches. Another of his appointments was as a representative of Indiana Yearly Meeting to the Indiana Council of Churches, along with

Carrie Davis, James Furbay, and William J. Sayers. Everywhere he worked as a pastor, he was active in the local ministerial association and/or the local council of churches.

The Social Order. As suggested throughout this volume, Dad was concerned with the soul of society as well as the souls of its citizens. He was not active in any political organization or any of the various reform groups (unless it was the League for Industrial Democracy in which he may have been a member.) He was interested in the cooperative movement, especially in the 1920s and 1930s, even though there were no co-op stores in the places where he was living at that time.

He did, however, keep abreast of political, social, and economic affairs. He read with keen interest the books written by men like Sherwood Eddy and Kirby Page, exponents of the social gospel. He devoured the magazine, *The World Tomorrow,* edited by Page, and *Fellowship,* the organ of the Fellowship of Reconciliation. He was an avid radio fan from the time he built his own little "crystal set" to the days when radio was far more advanced. Every evening he would listen to the broadcasts of Lowell Thomas right through to his famous "So long until tomorrow" sign-off.

He wove this knowledge and concern into his talks and sermons. He seldom repeated his illustrations, but several times he told about his visit to the Cadbury factory in England, the plant of the famous English Quaker chocolate-makers, and their pioneering efforts to fit their employees into the right jobs and to provide adequate living accommodations for them. More than once he referred to the attempts of people like J.C. Penney to apply their Christianity in their business dealings. In the 1920 election he voted for the Democrat, James Cox of Ohio, because he supported the League of Nations, whereas Warren G. Harding did not.

One day he returned from the visit with his friend Francis Jenkins, a Richmond-born inventor, and showed me some tiny photographs which were a part of his pioneering work on television. More than once Dad told the story of the banner in Jenkins' laboratory which proclaimed, "They said it couldn't be done, but Jenkins, poor fool, went ahead and did it." To Dad that was an illustration of the point that it was incumbent on Christians at times to attempt the seemingly impossible—the thing people said "just couldn't be done."

Legislation. Because of his strong belief that Christians should take part in politics, Murray Kenworthy was active as a citizen and as a member of at least four groups which pressed for legislation at the state or national levels. Those four were the Peace Association of Friends in America, the National Council for the Prevention of War, the American

Friends Service Committee, and the Friends Committee on National Legislation.

The FCNL grew out of the work of Ray Newton, Raymond Wilson, and others in the peace section of the American Friends Service Committee. Their efforts to influence legislation in Washington had threatened the tax-exempt status of the AFSC, and so it was decided to form a separate organization, devoted exclusively to lobbying in Washington.

The FCNL was formed at a conference in Richmond, Indiana, in June, 1938. That group selected Murray Kenworthy as the first chairman. He was well qualified for that position because of his knowledge of Quakers in the East and Midwest and because of his previous work in Washington with Frederic J. Libby in the National Council for the Prevention of War, a forerunner of the FCNL. Raymond Wilson was chosen as executive secretary.

His writings. Dad did not particularly enjoy writing. Nevertheless, he realized that he could reach a much wider audience in that way than through sermons and talks at various Quaker gatherings. So he exerted an extra effort from time to time to write.

Frequently he prepared material for *The Penn Quarterly* or *The Penn Teachers Quarterly* on the biblical background for use in Sunday School lessons for adults, or the section on the application of the lesson in everyday activities. Probably he reached the largest audience of his life through those notes in the publications of the Five Years Meeting.

He also wrote several pamphlets which were distributed by Indiana Yearly Meeting or the Five Years Meeting. They included these titles: *What Is Quakerism: Friends and the Sacraments; But I Say Unto You: A Discussion of the Bases of Christian Pacifism; Six Study Outlines for Young Friends Today; Preparation Course for Membership with Friends; What Do You Mean-Stewardship?;* and *The Rural Church in Indiana Yearly Meeting.*

He also wrote frequent articles in *The Messenger of Peace*, the publication of the Peace Association of Friends in America. After the death of Walter C. Woodward, Murray was asked to take over that editing responsibility. He did so reluctantly, as he had had little experience. Walter Woodward had been a veteran journalist as well as an historian. Murray thought that appointment would be for a few weeks, but it continued for eight months.

FINAL
YEARS

Finally, at the age of 72, Dad retired from active service for the Religious Society of Friends, and he and Mother settled down on the sixteen-acre plot in New London, Indiana, known as the Cosand place. The roots of both of them were in that small Quaker community where they had been born, had attended the local elementary and high school, and been active in the Friends Meeting.

The Cosand Place was on a splendid location at the edge of town. The small frame house was perched on the top of a hill, and the hillside and Honey Creek below it were guarded by sycamores and maples. Much of that small farm had once been an orchard, and several fruit trees were still standing when Dad and Mother went to live there. Nearby were two medium sized fields which were farmed by a neighbor.

Throughout most of her life Nora Cosand, Mother's sister, had lived there. She, too, had graduated from Earlham College and then taught for a short time in the Vermilion (Friends) Academy in Eastern Illinois. But she had returned to take care of her parents, and had remained there. Now Dad and Mother joined her.

How grateful they were for the many experiences of their lives. How glad to be relieved of so much traveling, so many problems, and so much responsibility. Their home was often called Orchard Knoll or Hilltop. But sometimes they referred to it fittingly as "Dunroven."

Just before they retired, or soon after that event, Dad and Mother were asked to go for a few months to teach at the boys and girls schools in Ramallah, Palestine, which were administered by Friends. Ramallah is ten miles north of Jerusalem. The schools had been founded by Eli and Sybil Jones, the uncle and aunt of Rufus Jones. Dad would do some teaching and serve as the part-time pastor of the small Friends meeting there.

It would have been a fitting culmination of their lives. Dad would have reveled in visiting all the places connected with the Bible and with the journeys of Jesus. Mother would have found enough to inspire her for the remainder of her life, transposing their experiences into poems, plays, and pageants. It is one of the few regrets I have that they did not see their way clear to go. But they had planned for many years to retire in New London and had looked forward to their later years there.

Retirement does not always mean a quiet, relaxed, peaceful period in one's life. Often it means a change of locality, a change of jobs, and a change of pace. People are wrong when they assume that older men and women have little to do. Occasionally that is true; often it is not.

Dad was available and was glad to be asked to help individuals, committees, and groups here and there. The Friends meeting in Kokomo needed someone to fill in for a short time, and he answered their call for help willingly. Then the New Salem Friends Meeting not many miles from New London needed a minister for several months. Dad and Mother drove there on Sundays for approximately two years and found that group especially congenial. There also were calls to serve on quarterly and yearly meeting committees and to speak from time to time to various Quaker conferences. Dad welcomed such opportunities.

I have a strong suspicion that Dad would like to have served here for a few months as the pastor of his old home meeting. But he was never asked. Perhaps the local group thought he would decline, and so never gave him the chance to reply. Probably some of them felt he was too old, especially to work with the young people. Undoubtedly a few thought he was not evangelical enough, too highbrow and learned, and/or too radical socially and politically. Nevertheless Dad served faithfully and helpfully on numerous local meeting committees and sometimes taught the men's class of the Sunday School. Occasionally he took part in the open period of the meeting for worship, and often he was asked to pronounce the benediction. One Friend once told me when I was vacationing at New London that those brief prayers often equaled in inspiration the twenty-to thirty-minute sermons of the pastor.

Retirement gave Dad the opportunity to carry out two distinct contributions locally. One was to plant a variety of trees in the large meetinghouse yard and in the ravine nearby, making it a small arboretum. That was a chance for him to foster his long interest in trees, to beautify the meeting property, and to give enjoyment to many people who came there for family reunions and other gatherings.

New London had long served as the site for the quarterly meeting burial ground, and although two large plots were kept in excellent shape, the oldest section was overgrown with weeds, briars, and small trees. Furthermore, many of the old gravestones had toppled from their foundation and were in disrepair. So he launched a project to restore that area, with several men and boys assisting him.

Some of the time he devoted to repairing the house and farm building on the Cosand place. For years there had not been a man there regularly to do such work; consequently there was plenty to do. He also needed to work on the hillside and on the bottom fields where thistles and daisies had almost choked out the corn, wheat, and soybeans that were planted there. In order to avoid the heat of the day, he would rise very early and walk down the hill to wage war against those "enemies," armed with his special weapons—a scythe, a sickle, a hoe, and a mattock. How he detested those weeds!

After dinner Dad and Mother often sat in the swing on the front porch and talked about their families, their friends, their travels, or what they had been reading. Or they would sit quietly and watch the squirrels, the birds—and the rabbits. sometimes Dad kept his rifle on his knees, ready to attack the rabbits which molested their garden and their flowers. That was the only "violence" in which Dad took a part as an adult. Often Dad and Mother would follow the lights of the automobiles as they moved along the road in front of their house, with the glow from them reflected on the nearby trees. Such were some of the dividends from their life-long investment in people and groups in many parts of the world. Such were some of the rich rewards of retirement.

Late in August of 1951 Dad had some physical difficulties, and he was taken to the Methodist Hospital in Indianapolis for a thorough examination. It seemed as if he was recovering enough that mother could return to New London. But then was stricken with pneumonitis, and other complications set in. Instead of recovering, he soon died. Mother always felt that he had had some premonition of his death; he had taught her to wind the clocks before he left for Indianapolis, a task which he had always done himself.

The memorial service was held in the Friends Meeting House in New London and was planned as the family thought he would have wanted it to be conducted. The local minister, Lyle Love, was in charge, and with him sat Ramey Taylor, the chairman of the Committee on Ministry and Oversight, and Glenn Reece, the executive secretary of Western Yearly Meeting.

It was a bitter, wintry day with icy roads, but the room was filled with relatives and friends from Indianapolis, Richmond, Muncie, Kokomo, Amboy, New Salem, and elsewhere. There were flowers from many others to whom Murray Kenworthy and his life and messages had meant much. After a few hymns and a message from Glenn Reece, there was an extended period of silence. Without doubt it was filled with prayers of thanksgiving for the life of Murray Kenworthy.

There were two messages I recall vividly which arose from the silence of that gathered meeting. One was the message of Carroll Kenworthy—words of appreciation for the part that the New London Meeting and community had played in a long and useful life, equipping him well for the race he had run. The other was a message from Norman Young, the pastor of the Friends meeting in Kokomo, expressing appreciation for Murray's vision and contributions to the wider world of Friends and others.

Dad was buried, then, in the New London Cemetery, next to Mamma, and near his father, his mother, and his stepmother. The tributes to him soon began to pour in. Perhaps excerpts from a few will help readers to grasp the high regard in which he had been held by individuals and groups.

From the American Friends Service Committee came a Minute which said:

> The Board expressed its deep sympathy in the recent passing of Murray S. Kenworthy and wishes to record its gratitude for the many valuable contributions he has made to the work of the American Friends Service Committee, particularly the service he undertook for it after the First World War.

In a letter from Merle L. Davis, the Administrative Secretary of the American Friends Board of Mission, he reported on a Minute from that group, pointing out that:

> For 15 years he served as a member of the American Friends Board of Missions....With the exception of the four years between 1931 and 1934, he served continuously until his retirement in 1945. He was on the Executive Committee and chairman of the Candidates Committee for the last 10 years of

that time and on two occasions he served as acting secretary during the absence of the secretary on trips to Kenya and Palestine.

It is impossible to enumerate all of the activites and interests of Murray Kenworthy for he had a vital concern for the work of every department of the Five Years Meeting and was always willing to lend a helping hand wherever he was needed.

Added to the more formal Minute was Merle Davis' comment:

Murray was one of the men whom I have appreciated deeply in connection with the work of the mission board and I enjoyed trips with him from time to time as well as appreciating the advice and suggestions which he offered graciously from time to time.

Howard Cope, the pastor of the large Friends Memorial Church in Muncie, Indiana, and a close personal friend of Dad's, wrote:

Murray was a man from whom I often sought counsel and upon whose word and loyalty I could always depend. Our association has very greatly enriched my life, and I thank the Heavenly Father for what he meant to us.

Harold Chance, one of the leading proponents of the peace testimony of Friends all over the United States, wrote:

Murray was a mighty good man and a mighty effective one. Through the years I have known him, he has been a real inspiration to me and to many others.

And Glenn Reece, the executive secretary of Western Yearly Meeting, said in a personal letter to me:

Your father has long been a source of great inspiration to me, and that has increased steadily as our acquaintance and friendship has grown. His counsel, always freely shared when sought, had been extremely helpful at many points in my life and in any credit which may come to me in the future for my work, a goodly portion shall be his.

Mother lived for several years after Dad, first at the family place in New London and then in a retirement home in Fort Wayne. She died at the age of 96. She, too was a "minister", but her ministry was very different from Dad's. Of all her characteristics, I think the outstanding one was that she listened with love. She seldom gave advice and never unless it was sought directly. But the cars kept coming up the lane at Hilltop, Orchard Knoll, or Dunroven, so that people could talk with her. Almost always they went away feeling better about themselves and better able to cope with whatever had been on their minds when they came.

Born in a small community in New London, Indiana, Dad had a wealth of experiences, many of which broadened his horizons. He did indeed live in a larger world than most people, throughout his life. Then he returned "home" to New London near the end of his many useful years. He had run a good race; he had finished the course. The world was better for his sojourn here.

APPENDIX

Developments in the United States and in American Quakerdom	Murray S. Kenworthy's Related Activities
Migration of Quakers into Indiana a. Establishment of meetings b. Founding of schools and academies	Settlement of New London, Indiana as a Quaker community a. New London Monthly and Quarterly Meetings b. New London Friends School and Academy
The formation of public high schools	New London Friends Academy becomes a public high school
Rise of the pastoral system among Friends	New London Meeting gradually becomes a semi-programmed meeting
Development of Quaker Colleges	Friends Boarding School becomes Earlham College; Murray Kenworthy as a student
1902 Most Orthodox friends unite to form Five Years Meeting	Murray Kenworthy as the youngest delegate and clerk of the Western Yearly Meeting delegation
Difficulties among Christians in the U.S.A. over evolution and higher criticism	Attack on Murray Kenworthy's teaching at Earlham College: his ouster
A Few Quaker ministers begin to obtain special education for their work	Murray Kenworthy at the Harvard Divinity School; awarded S.T.B.
The world-wide Society of Friends begins to form	Attends First World Conference of Friends in England
World War I	Censure in Glens Falls, N.Y. as a pacifist; heads first C.O. camp; Works for the AFSC
Post-war disturbances in Europe and famine in the Soviet Union	Directs Quaker famine relief work in the Soviet Union

Decline of many farm communities;
    migration to the cities

Quaker work to strengthen midwestern
    Quakerism

Concern for more unity among American
    Quakers

Concern for rural churches of Friends;
    heads Rural Life Association

Secretary of Wilmington Yearly Meeting
    and then of Indiana Yearly Meeting

Attends All Friends Conference at Penn
    College in 1929

Works with various groups of Friends in
    the Washington, D.C. Meeting

Visits among different groups of Quakers

Some Special Concerns of Friends
    A. Education

Attends Earlham College; teaches at
    Earlham and Wilmington Colleges

Sends sons to Oakwood and Westtown

Urges young Quakers to go to college

    B. Peace

Active in the Peace Association of Friends
    in America and other groups

Quaker representative on Historic Peace
    Churches Committee

Works with Frederick J. Libby in the
    National Council for the Prevention
    of War.

Work with the AFSC

    C. Service

Heads AFSC work in the Soviet Union
    and forms Midwest Regional Office of
    the AFSC

    D. Missions

Long-time member of the American Board
    of Missions

    E. Religious education

Work in various meetings; writes for
    young people and Sunday Schools;
    work at Quaker Haven

Development of the World Society of
    Friends

Delegate to the First and Second World
    Conferences of Friends in England and
    in the United States.

Aids in formation of the Friends World
    Committee for Consultation

Interest in the education of Quaker
    ministers and pastors

Develops training courses in Wilmington
    and Indiana Yearly Meetings. Takes
    part in early discussion on the
    formation of the Earlham School of
    Religion

NOTES FOR FUTURE HISTORIANS

The preparation of this book has been a labor of love as a tribute from Murray S. Kenworthy's youngest son, Leonard Stout Kenworthy, aided and abetted by his other two sons–Carroll Holloway Kenworthy and Wilmer Edwards Kenworthy. As such the research and writing of this volume has been a fascinating undertaking. Through that work I have learned much about several topics–such as life in Indiana in the latter part of the nineteenth century, the history of Earlham College, midwestern Quakerism, conditions in the USSR in the early 1920s, and other subjects. In the process I think I have learned much about my father, our Kenworthy family–and even myself.

Nevertheless, it has been at times a baffling and frustrating experience as the souces for such a volume have been so scarce. For example, I had always thought that very little had been written about Quaker education in Indiana, about the early years of the Five Years Meeting, and about programmed and semi-programmed Friends Meetings. Now I am certain that that is true. Hence I want to encourage younger people to delve more deeply into these and related topics than I have been able to do in the amount of time I allotted to this undertaking. There are many such subjects for future Quaker historians to study. For such persons and for the readers who are interested in the documentation I used for this book, I want to record what I found.

The three general histories that I have found useful have been Errol Elliott's *Quakers on the American Frontier: A History of the Westward Migrations, Settlements, and Developments of Friends on the American Continent* (Richmond, Indiana: Friends United Press, 1969.); Elbert Russell's *The History of Quakerism* (New York: Macmillian, 1942. 586 pp. and a recent reprint by the Friends United Press); and Allen C. Thomas' *A History of Friends in America* (Philadelphia: John C. Winston, 1919. 285 pp.). Unfortunately Howard Brinton's *Friends for 300 Years* (New York: Harper, 1952. 239 pp.) has very little to say on the topics about which I was doing research.

For the first two chapters I have relied heavily on an account of his life which Murray Kenworthy began to write at the request of his sons just before his death. Six chapters had been written in rough draft. They are full of fascinating material, but far too detailed to use for the average reader.

On life in Richmond, Indiana, I used Daisy Marvel Jones' *Richmond: Eastern Gateway to Indiana* (Richmond, Indiana: Richmond Public School 1959. 213 pp.), a popular account for elementary school children but nevertheless containing some important data. On a few points I was able to use Howard H. Peckham's *Indiana: A Bicentennial History* (New York: Norton, 1978. 207 pp.). The Wayne County Historical Society kindly answered some of the questions I posed about that place and that period of history.

On Earlham College the fullest account is to be found in Opal Thornburg's *Earlham: The Story of a College: 1847-1962* (Richmond, Indiana: The Earlham College Press, 1963. 484 pp.) In it and in Ethel Hittle McDaniel's brochure on *The Contribution of the Society of Friends to Education in Indiana* (Indianapolis: Indiana Historical Society, 1939. 112pp.) I found some valuable material on the various Quaker academies in that state in the nineteenth century and even into the twentieth century. Some additional background was obtained from these three volumes: *Elbert Russell: Quaker: An Autobiography* (Jackson, Tennessee: Friendly Press, 1956. 376 pp.), *Autobiography of Allen Jay* (Philadelphia; John C. Winston Company, 1908. 421 pp.), and Walter C. Woodward's *Timothy Nicholson: Master Quaker: A Biography* (Richmond, Indiana: Nicholson Press, 1927. 252 pp.). In addition, I have had the personal recollections of Caroline Nicholson Jacob, Carroll Kenworthy, Florence Mills, and S. Francis Nicholson, all of whom were either in Earlham as students or connected with Earlham in the period of Murray Kenworthy's years there.

On the Harvard years the best book for this account was Walter Rauschenbusch's *Christianity and the Social Crisis* (New York: George H. Doran Company, 1907. 429 pp.).

For the chapter on Glens Falls, New York and Wilmington, Ohio I relied in part on the *Minutes* of Wilmington Yearly Meeting, plus recollections of the Kenworthy family.

Documentation on the relief work done by Quakers in the Soviet Union is much more ample. The fullest account is Richenda A. Scott's *Quakers in Russia* (London: Michael Joseph, 1964. 302 pp.). Other valuable background came from A. Ruth Fry's *A Quaker Adventure* (New York, Fran-Maurice, Undated. 389 pp.), John Ormerod Greenwood's *Quaker Encounters: Volume I: Friends and Relief* (York, England: Sessions Ltd.) Mary Hoxie Jones' *Swords Into Ploughshares: An Account of the American Friends Service Committee: 1917-1937* (New York: Macmillian, 1937. 374 pp.), and Lester M. Jones' *Quakers In Action: Recent Humanitarian and Reform Activities of the American Quakers* (New York: Macmillian, 1929. 226 pp.). A stack of letters from Murray Kenworthy to his family and some materials in the archives of the American Friends Service Committee were invaluable.

From that point on much of the material is taken from the recollections I have of the life of Murray Kenworthy, plus a few items kept by his family. On the chapter on the establishment of the Midwest regional office of the AFSC, there was a folder from Murray Kenworthy's files, plus some material in the archives of the American Friends Service Committee in Philadelphia.

On the Amboy and Carthage periods in Murray Kenworthy's life I was aided by personal correspondence with a few friends in those places who lived there when he was pastor. I want to thank Lola Prout in particular for obtaining brief comments from people in the Amboy Friends Meeting.

For the period when Murray Kenworthy was executive secretary of Indiana Yearly Meeting, his annual reports in the *Minutes* of that body were especially helpful.

The remaining parts of this book were based in large part on my personal memories, plus the letters which came to members of the Kenworthy family at the time of Murray Kenworthy's death.